CLASSROOM EXPERIMENTS

To Accompany Taylor's *Economics:*
A User's Guide

Greg Delemeester
Marietta College

and

John Neral
Frostburg State University

Editor-in-Chief: Bonnie Binkert
Editorial Assistant: Tamela Ambush
Senior Manufacturing Coordinator: Priscilla J. Bailey
Marketing Manager: Charles Baker

Cover Design: Harold Burch, Harold Burch Design, NYC

Copyright © 1995 by Houghton Mifflin Company. All rights reserved.

Permission is hereby granted to teachers to reprint or photocopy this work or portions thereof in classroom quantities for use in their classes with accompanying Houghton Mifflin material, provided each copy made shows the copyright notice. If more than ten (10) copies are made, this copyright page and statement of restrictions should be included. No fee may be collected for such copies beyond the cost of duplicating and further distribution is expressly prohibited. Except as authorized above, prior written permission must be obtained from Houghton Mifflin Company to reproduce or transmit this work or portions thereof in any other form or by any other electronic or mechanical means, including any information storage or retrieval system, unless expressly permitted by federal copyright law. Address inquiries to College Permissions, Houghton Mifflin Company, 222 Berkeley Street, Boston, MA 02116-3764

Printed in the U.S.A.

ISBN: 0-395-74421-0

123456789-PR-99 98 97 96 95

PREFACE

In *ECONOMICS*, John Taylor has written a text which features the growing use of experimental methods by economists in their quest to understand how and why an economy works as it does. This manual contains eighteen experiments designed to help students better understand economic concepts. We believe that classroom experiments provide the student with the opportunity to actively view an economic model from the inside, as opposed to viewing the model passively from the outside as is often the case with the traditional lecture approach.

Most of the experiments included here came our way through a newsletter, *Classroom Expernomics*, which we initiated back in 1992 after attending a workshop on the classroom uses of experimental economics sponsored by the National Science Foundation at the University of Arizona. Several other experiments have been adapted from those that have appeared in research journals or those that we have invented ourselves.

The majority of the experiments contained in this manual pertain to microeconomic topics, as most of the early experimental research has tended to focus on individual and market behavior. There does appear, though, to be a growing number of economists using experiments to test and refine various macroeconomic models.

Each experiment has been edited to fit our format. In some cases, we have taken the liberty of adding elements not included in the original contributions, such as review questions and suggestions for further reading. We trust that our colleagues will not find our additions and/or deletions inimical to their original work.

Each experimental description begins with an overview of the fundamental economic concepts to be demonstrated, followed by a list of any materials necessary to implement the experiment. The next section provides a step-by-step set of instructions for administering the experiment in the classroom. A discussion section follows pointing out the expected (and sometimes unexpected) results of the experiment. Suggestions for variations of the experimental design may also be included here. Subsequent sections include discussion questions (and suggested answers), suggestions for further reading, and appendices containing instructions for students and any necessary forms.

ACKNOWLEDGMENTS

Our interest in experimental economics was initially sparked during our graduate school days and later reignited at the National Science Foundation workshops on experimental economics at the University of Arizona. For that initial spark, we owe a debt of gratitude to our mentors, Raymond Battalio of Texas A&M University and Jack Ochs of the University of Pittsburgh. We also thank Donald Wells of the University of Arizona and Arlington Williams of Indiana University for the efforts that they have put forth over the past several years in spreading the word about classroom experiments in the NSF workshops.

We are especially grateful to our colleagues who have contributed their experiments to this manual. We also extend our thanks to everyone who has contributed to our newsletter, *Classroom Expernomics*, where many of the experiments contained in this manual first appeared. To Nomi Sofer and Ann West of Houghton Mifflin we offer our thanks for their many helpful suggestions. We would also like to thank Jennifer Warnick and Nikki Brown for their help in putting together this manual.

Finally, we would like to thank our respective families for putting up with two experimental economists (though hopefully not experimental husbands and fathers).

TABLE OF CONTENTS

Preface ... iii
Acknowledgments ... iv
Suggested Schedule of Experiments ... vi

Experiments in the Classroom: An Introduction ... 1
Experiment 1: An Experimental Derivation
    of the Production Possibilities Curve ... 5
Experiment 2: A Comparative Advantage Experiment ... 12
Experiment 3: The Experimental Derivation
    of a Market Demand Curve ... 19
Experiment 4: The Double Oral Auction ... 22
Experiment 5: The Double Oral Auction with
    Price Controls/Taxes ... 37
Experiment 6: The Posted Offer Auction ... 51
Experiment 7: Widget Production and Cost ... 61
Experiment 8: The Dollar Auction ... 66
Experiment 9: A Price-Searching Experiment ... 69
Experiment 10: Oligopoly, Interdependence, and Collusion (I) ... 77
Experiment 11: Oligopoly, Interdependence, and Collusion (II) ... 85
Experiment 12: The Prisoner's Dilemma ... 90
Experiment 13: An Experimental Test of Preferences Over
    the Distribution of Income ... 93
Experiment 14: A Public Goods Experiment ... 100
Experiment 15: A Pollution Rights Trading Game ... 107
Experiment 16: The Coase Theorem ... 115
Experiment 17: Beans as a Medium of Exchange ... 120
Experiment 18: A Double Oral Auction Bond Market Experiment ... 125
Bibliography ... 131

SUGGESTED SCHEDULE OF EXPERIMENTS

Experiment	Primary Application Chapter in Taylor's *Economics*	Secondary Application Chapter(s) in Taylor's *Economics*
Experiment 1: An Experimental Derivation of the Production Possibilities Curve	2	
Experiment 2: A Comparative Advantage Experiment	2	18
Experiment 3: The Experimental Derivation of a Market Demand Curve	3	5
Experiment 4: The Double Oral Auction	7	1,3,4,13,16,19
Experiment 5: The Double Oral Auction with Price Controls/Taxes	7	3,15
Experiment 6: The Posted Offer Auction	7	10,11
Experiment 7: Widget Production and Cost	8	6
Experiment 8: The Dollar Auction	8	6
Experiment 9: A Price-Searching Experiment	10	
Experiment 10: Oligopoly, Interdependence, and Collusion (I)	11	
Experiment 11: Oligopoly, Interdependence, and Collusion (II)	11	
Experiment 12: The Prisoner's Dilemma	11	
Experiment 13: An Experimental Test of Preferences over the Distribution of Income	15	
Experiment 14: A Public Goods Experiment	16	
Experiment 15: A Pollution Rights Trading Game	16	
Experiment 16: The Coase Theorem	16	
Experiment 17: Beans as a Medium of Exchange	26	
Experiment 18: A Double Oral Auction Bond Market Experiment	26	13

EXPERIMENTS IN THE CLASSROOM: AN INTRODUCTION

SOME BENEFITS AND COSTS OF DOING EXPERIMENTS

The use of laboratory experiments is an exciting and relatively new technique for most economists, in terms of both research and pedagogy.[1] In the classroom, experiments require students to participate actively as subjects under a variety of simulated market settings to help them understand how incentives and constraints directly affect behavior. Learning economics through the use of algebraic and graphical models via lecture is setting-specific: students generally cannot apply the theories outside of the specific graphs and algebraic models used in the classroom. Indeed, Wells (1991) has observed:

> The use of economic experiments in instruction enables students to experience the functioning of markets and to discover principles of economics in a laboratory setting. If the equilibrium price emerges from the actions of student participants in a double oral auction experiment, the credibility of other theoretical models is substantially enhanced, even when these models are presented without using experiments.

The use of classroom experiments may also give your students an appreciation for how the scientific method is used to address economic questions. For example, although statistical procedures such as regression analysis may be beyond the understanding of most principles students, experiments can be a good means of introducing them to the various empirical procedures employed by economists. Experiments can also reinforce the conditional (*ceteris paribus*) nature of economic models.

The implementation of classroom experiments does involve some significant opportunity costs. First, there are start-up costs when a particular experiment is implemented for the first time. Materials for running the experiment must be generated, and experimental procedures must be learned. One of the primary goals of this manual is to minimize these costs by providing 1) an easily replicable set of materials for each of the experiments we describe, and 2) a clear and reasonably concise description of the procedures. For most instructors, however, the most important opportunity cost is the lecture time that must be sacrificed in order to introduce experiments into the classroom. Although some instructors view classroom experiments as a substitute for the classroom lecture, we consider most of the experiments in this manual to be complements to classroom lectures. Consequently, instructors who use classroom experiments often find themselves sacrificing some topic coverage to accommodate

---

[1] See Davis and Holt (1993) and Friedman and Sunder (1994) for a thorough discussion of the research aspects of experimental economics; see the Fall 1993 issue of the *Journal of Economic Education* for a more thorough discussion of the pedagogical aspects of experimental economics.

the experiments. In the end, we suspect that the decision of whether or not to utilize classroom experiments is a choice between breadth of topic coverage and depth of student understanding.

BEFORE YOU RUN AN EXPERIMENT

As a general rule, we prefer to run an experiment prior to our classroom presentation of the relevant theory/material. We do this for several reasons. First, we do not wish to influence how the students should behave. Second, the explanatory power of the relevant theory will have a bigger impact on the students if at first they are unaware of its implications.[2]

We also strongly suggest that all experiments be followed by an appropriate debriefing session. For some experiments, such as the double oral auction, a culminating lab report to be completed by the student may be appropriate. In any case, the instructor should stress the linkage between the relevant economic theory and the data generated by the experiment.

Most of the experiments in this manual are designed for class sizes of thirty or forty students. Instructors teaching larger classes can also utilize these experiments, either by selecting a subset of students to participate and having the other students simply observe or by dividing the class into groups with each group participating in its own market. Instructors adopting the latter approach would certainly require additional help (teaching assistants, perhaps) in conducting and monitoring the several, simultaneous markets.

All of the experiments in this manual are designed to be run manually. That is, they can be run in a standard classroom without the use of computers or other more sophisticated equipment. Although you should be able to run most of these experiments in a normal fifty-minute class period (or a portion thereof), some may require that you conduct a debriefing in the following class period. For those who have ready access to computer facilities, some of the experiments described here have computerized versions. Computerized experiments have the advantage of speedier operation and data storage/retrieval capacities. In some cases, a networked system of PCs is required to run the software. If a particular experiment has been computerized, that fact is noted in the description of the experiment.

In planning some of these experiments, you must make a few basic decisions. First, how many students will participate in the experiment? Although in some experiments the entire class more or less automatically participates, in many others this decision will determine the answers to several logistical questions such as the number of forms required and the setup of the classroom. The number of participants is a critical factor in the design of experiments like the double oral auction (see Experiment 4). On occasion, you will find that on the day of the experiment the anticipated number of students do not appear in class. To compensate for this possibility, one can plan for a slightly smaller than normal class attendance and utilize any "extra" students as lab assistants.

---

[2]Before conducting the double oral auction, some instructors, known for their flair for the dramatic, have held up envelopes proclaiming to contain the predicted prices and exchange quantities. Upon completing the experiment, the instructor then opens the envelope and reveals the (correct) predictions to an amazed classroom.

Another important decision is whether or not to offer any motivational incentives to students based on their performance in the experiment.[3] For research experiments, cash payments are almost always used to induce the desired preferences.[4] In such experiments, a general rule of thumb is to ensure that the average student subject earns something close to the going wage on campus.

For instructors doing experiments in the classroom, however, the use of money as a motivational incentive may not be a feasible option given the obvious financial constraints. Indeed, money may not even be a dominant reward mechanism from the students' point of view. It is our experience that what seems to get most students' attention is the chance to accumulate grade points. Points can be allocated either as part of a bonus system or as a regular part of the classroom grade calculation. In either case, the instructor must be convinced that the grade points measure some element of student learning (Friedman and Sunder, 1994). In general, though, it is probably wise to restrict the portion of a course grade that depends on a student's performance in classroom experiments to a small fraction of the overall grade.

As one example of how to utilize bonus points, consider the following system used by Williams and Walker (1993). In their version of the public goods experiment (our Experiment 14), a transformed performance index based on an individual's relative earnings is used. Thus:

$$\text{Performance Index} = \frac{i\text{'s actual earnings} - i\text{'s minimum possible earnings}}{i\text{'s max possible earnings} - i\text{'s min possible earnings}}$$

The index ranges from 0 to 1 for each individual. Williams and Walker multiplied each person's index by 3 and added it to the student's final grade average. Thus the extra credit range was 0 - 3 points.

In their version of the price searching experiment (our Experiment 9), Williams and Walker use a tournament structure for determining a rank score, which is then transformed into bonus points. Each participant's accumulated profits are ranked relative to the accumulated profits of other participants according to the following scale:

Top third of the class:	6 rank points
Middle third of the class:	4 rank points
Bottom third of the class:	2 rank points

The rank score is then added to the student's final course average.

---

[3] In his seminal work on laboratory methods in economics, Smith (1982) argues that an appropriate motivational medium should satisfy three conditions: nonsatiation, salience, and dominance. Nonsatiation requires that the student subjects prefer more of the reward medium to less. Salience requires that student subjects realize a linkage between their decisions and their payoffs. Dominance requires that the reward mechanism outweigh any other possible motivational objective that student subjects may hold (such as pleasing the instructor).

[4] Friedman and Sunder (1994) provide a general discussion of the use of monetary rewards in the conduct of research experiments.

A variety of other reward mechanisms have been employed by instructors utilizing experiments in the classroom. Among these are payments-in-kind (usually food items such as candy bars, soft drinks, etc.), which are based on a tournament structure as just described. You could also use a point system whereby students accumulate points that are then applied toward a class raffle or lottery in which a prize (an economics textbook?) will be given away. Finally, we have also relied on the inherent fun of participating in such experiments to motivate our students to do their best. You should also not be surprised at your students' willing and enthusiastic participation just for learning's sake.

A final preliminary step that you might want to take is to inquire about your campus's rules regarding the use of student subjects in classroom "laboratory experiments." Many colleges have a Human Subjects Committee that monitors the ethical treatment of human subjects in research experiments and often requires that consent forms be obtained from such subjects. Although you probably won't run into any problems with such a committee, it's wise to check ahead of time.

Before you begin any experiment, we urge you to review all student instructions aloud and in front of the entire class to reduce the likelihood of misunderstanding. The less misunderstanding among your students about what they must do, the less likely your experiment will generate unexpected (and difficult to explain) results.

Finally, have fun. Experiments are an exciting means of communicating economic theories to students. If they are carefully administered and followed up with good discussions, experiments can be a meaningful learning experience for all (including the instructor).

REFERENCES

Davis, Douglas D., and Charles Holt. Experimental Economics. Princeton University Press, 1993.

Friedman, Daniel, and Shyam Sunder. Experimental Methods: A Primer for Economists. Cambridge University Press, 1994.

Smith, Vernon. "Microeconomic Systems as an Experimental Science." American Economic Review (December 1982): 923-955.

Wells, Donald A. "Laboratory Experiments for Undergraduate Instruction in Economics." Journal of Economic Education (Summer 1991): 293-300.

Williams, Arlington W. and James M. Walker. "Computerized Laboratory Exercises for Microeconomics Education: Three Applications Motivated by Experimental Economics." Journal of Economic Education (Fall 1993): 291-315.

EXPERIMENT 1: AN EXPERIMENTAL DERIVATION OF THE PRODUCTION POSSIBILITIES CURVE

OVERVIEW

In many principles courses, scarcity and the related concept of opportunity cost are among the first economic concepts that students encounter. Because these concepts comprise the foundation for so much of the material that follows, it is extremely important that beginning students understand them thoroughly. The production possibilities curve, our primary analytical tool for illustrating the concept of scarcity, is for us both simple and elegant. But because many beginning students have difficulty dealing with the high level of abstraction that permeates economic theory, they may have trouble relating the textbook treatment of scarcity to scarcity in the real world. The following exercise serves as a quick and entertaining means of providing students with a bit of experience with scarcity in a small (but real) economic system that must allocate its scarce resources between the production of two goods.[1]

MATERIALS NEEDED

- A work surface (half of the desk or table at the front of the classroom works fine)
- A stapler and supply of staples
- Paper (8.5" x 11" sheets that have been cut in half prior to class)
- Student worksheets for use in recording the production data and deriving the production possibilities curve

ADMINISTERING THE EXPERIMENT

First, distribute a copy of the handout (reproduced in the Appendices that follow) to each student. Then describe the nature of the resources that will be used during the experiment. The work surface, the paper, and the stapler constitute capital. Students will supply labor, which will be used in conjunction with this capital to produce two commodities, widgets and whajamas. A widget is produced by tearing a sheet of paper in half, folding it twice, and stapling it. A whajama is produced by folding a sheet of paper three times (no tearing, no stapling). Both widgets and whajamas are very fragile and break if they fall onto the floor at any time during the production process.

---

[1]This experiment is derived from Neral and Ray (1995).

At this point, ask five students to volunteer to supply labor.[2] Production of widgets and whajamas proceeds over a number of production periods of a set length (forty-five seconds is usually adequate). One unit of labor consists of one student working for one production period (that is, forty-five seconds). In each production period, the available capital and labor are allocated between the production of widgets and the production of whajamas in a different way. The stapler is allocated to either the widget industry or the whajama industry in each period and is normalized as $K = 1$. The work surface and the paper are always shared by the two industries (and hence do not have their own columns on the handout). In the first production period, all five units of labor and the stapler are allocated to the production of widgets. At the end of the production period, the number of widgets (and whajamas!) that have been produced is observed and recorded by students on the handout and by the instructor on the blackboard or a transparency (see the Appendices which follow). In the second production period, all five units of labor and the stapler are allocated to the production of whajamas. At the end of the production period, the number of whajamas (and widgets!) that have been produced is observed and recorded. In the remaining production periods, the stapler is allocated to the widget industry, while labor is allocated between widget and whajama production in various ways. At the end of each period, the number of units of each commodity produced during the period is recorded.

At the end of the final production period, the combinations of widgets and whajamas produced under various allocations of resources can be graphed and used to infer the position of the production possibilities curve.

A word of caution is in order at this point. This exercise will usually, but not always, generate a production possibilities curve that is negatively sloped and concave to the origin. When the resulting production possibilities curve has a positively sloped section, it usually lies immediately adjacent to one of the axes and is usually the result of the less efficient production that occurs during the initial production period(s). After the first period (or two), students usually become more adept at producing the commodities. As a result, more widgets may be produced by three students during the final period than were produced by five students during the first period. When this occurs, the resulting upward-sloping portion of the production possibilities curve can usually be eliminated by repeating the allocation that was used in the initial period. The now more efficient students will usually generate enough additional output to generate a production possibilities curve with something resembling its smooth, downward-sloping textbook appearance.

DISCUSSION

By the end of this exercise, your students should have a much clearer understanding of the concepts of scarcity and opportunity cost, and of how these concepts can be illustrated using

---

[2] If you're patient, five students will eventually volunteer; if you're not the patient sort, simply draft five students. Since the lecture on scarcity usually occurs very early in the course, this exercise also serves as an excellent icebreaker. By the end of this exercise, most students will be somewhat less inhibited about participating in class discussions and/or exercises.

a production possibilities curve. The data can also be used to calculate the opportunity cost of an additional unit of either good between points on the curve.

This exercise provides a foundation for any subsequent discussion of economic growth. For example, if workers in the widget industry began to tear several sheets of paper in half at the same time (instead of one at a time), this technological progress would result in biased growth. There would be an increase in the number of widgets that could be produced with existing resources during a single production period and an outward shift of the production possibilities curve along the widget axis (but not along the whajama axis). An increase in the number of units of available labor would result in a more uniform outward shift of the production possibilities function. Although it is possible to introduce these variations into the exercise itself, we usually find it sufficient to suggest that they *might* be carried out, allowing students to speculate as to their effects on the position of the production possibilities curve.

QUESTIONS

1. Suppose that a technological improvement occurs in the widget industry: workers are instructed to tear several sheets of paper in half at the same time. How would this improvement affect the position of the production possibilities curve?

   [The technological advance should result in an increase in the number of widgets that can be produced with any given allocation of resources. Hence the production possibilities curve should shift outward along the widget axis.]

2. Suppose that the amount of available labor increases from five units of labor to seven units of labor. How would this affect the position of the production possibilities curve?

   [The increase in labor will make it possible to produce more widgets (if all resources are allocated to the widget industry), more whajamas (if all resources are allocated to the whajama industry), or more of both commodities (if the resources are allocated between the widgets and whajamas). Hence, the entire production possibilities curve should shift outward.]

REFERENCES/FURTHER READING

Neral, John, and Margaret Ray. "Experiential Learning in the Undergraduate Classroom: Two Exercises." Economic Inquiry (January 1995): 170-174.

APPENDICES TO EXPERIMENT 1

- Student worksheet to be distributed to students at the beginning of the exercise
- Transparency masters containing the same information as the handout

If you don't use transparencies, the information from the handout and the production possibilities curve can be placed on the blackboard.

Experimental Derivation of the Production Possibilities Curve 9

STUDENT WORKSHEET

SCARCITY, PRODUCTION POSSIBILITIES CURVES, TECHNOLOGY, AND GROWTH

Resources: paper and work surface, stapler ($K = 1$), labor ($L = 5$)
(All resources are fixed.)

To Produce:
1. Widgets: divide paper in half, fold twice, staple
2. Whajamas: fold paper three times

Resource allocations:

Allocation	Widgets (W1) K	L	W1	Whajamas (W2) K	L	W2
A	1	5	___	0	0	___
B	0	0	___	1	5	___
C	1	2	___	0	3	___
D	1	3	___	0	2	___

Use the data generated above to construct a production possibilities curve in the following graph.

Scarcity, Production Possibilities Curves, Technology, and Growth

Resources (all fixed):
1. Paper and work surface
2. Stapler ($K = 1$)
3. Labor ($L = 5$)

To Produce:
1. Widgets: divide paper in half, fold twice, staple
2. Whajamas: fold paper three times

Resource allocations:

| Widgets (W1) ||| Whajamas (W2) |||
K	L	W1	K	L	W2
1	5	___	0	0	___
0	0	___	1	5	___
1	2	___	0	3	___
1	3	___	0	2	___

W2

0   W1

EXPERIMENT 2: A COMPARATIVE ADVANTAGE EXPERIMENT

OVERVIEW

Paul Samuelson once said that David Ricardo's demonstration of comparative advantage is one piece of economics which is perfectly simple without being perfectly obvious. This is shown, he claims, by the many business and political leaders of obvious intelligence who have utterly failed to understand it.

Unfortunately, the same can also be said of the many intelligent economics students who, having learned to parrot the theory, still do not *believe* it. As an MBA student once said after seeing the Ricardian triangles presented on the blackboard, "Well, it's all theory, isn't it?"

The best response to such healthy skepticism is for students to take a ride atop those trade triangles themselves--before hearing what theory says should happen.[1]

MATERIALS NEEDED

- Graph paper (or prepared graphs) for each student
- Student worksheet

ADMINISTERING THE EXPERIMENT

Have your students pair up, letting them choose who will play the part of Mexico and who the United States. Then hand out graph paper and ask them to reproduce linear production possibilities curves for two goods, trucks and computers, as shown in Figure 1 (minus the points labeled *A* and *B*). Or, to speed things up, simply distribute copies of the figure to the students.[2]

Having explained what production possibilities curves are, ask each student to pick any point along his or her curve that he or she "likes"--the best point of production/consumption in autarky. Sample points are represented by points *A* and *B* in Figure 1.

---

[1] This is an edited version of an experiment that Jim Stodder contributed to the Spring, 1994, issue of *Classroom Expernomics*.

[2] Another more time-consuming (but learning-inducing) alternative is to provide students with a pair of linear equations that define the production possibilities curves. A final alternative is to provide students with a textbook-style table of labor requirements for the production of one computer and one truck in each country; if you also indicate the relative endowments of labor in each country, students will be able to derive the production possibilities curves.

Comparative Advantage

Now ask each pair of students, given these best autarkic points, if they can find a way to swap trucks and computers that makes each country better off. Explain that even without knowing anyone's preferences, we can still agree that a country is "better off" if it gets *no less of each* of the goods and *more of at least one* than under autarky. Thus the right-angled indifference curves in Figure 1. A student worksheet containing a number of descriptive questions to assist students in organizing their thoughts during the experiment is included among the Appendices at the end of the experiment.

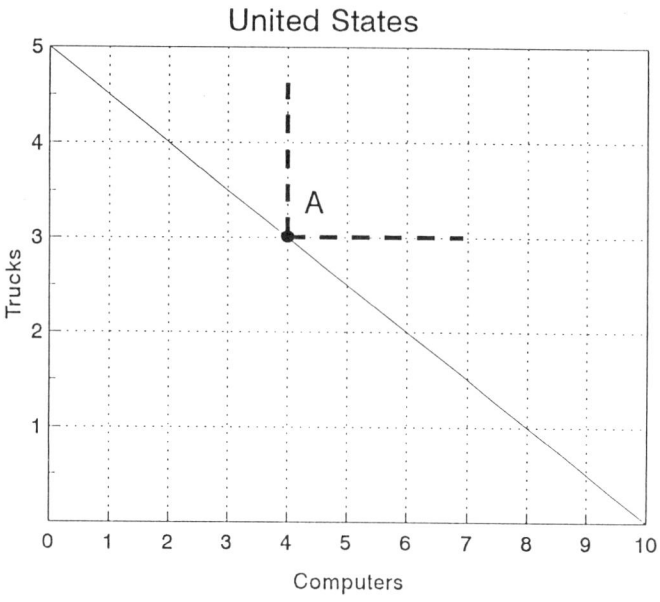

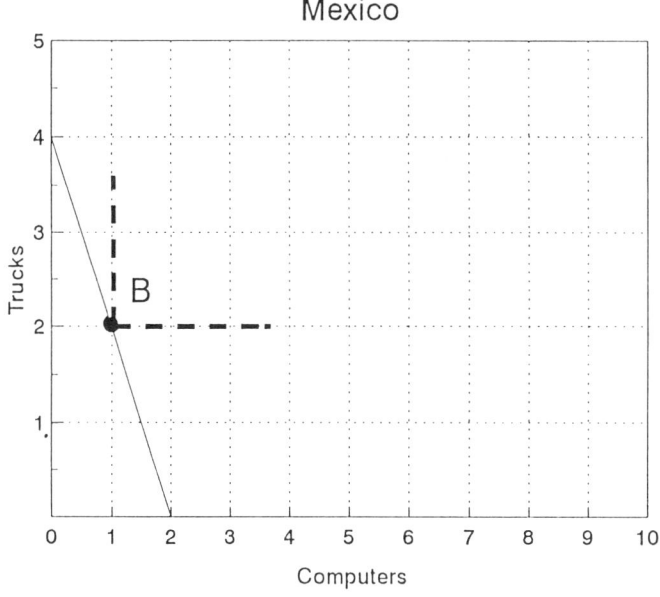

Figure 1

DISCUSSION

After approximately thirty minutes, about half the pairs will have figured it out. Students often settle on "1-for-1" terms of trade intermediate to their production possibilities curve slopes. In my experience involving classes of MBAs and freshmen, there was no real difference in this rate of discovery between MBAs and freshmen--thus confirming Samuelson's point. A couple of student comments are worth noting.

Sometimes the students playing the role of the United States will say, "How can you make me better off? I can do both things better than you!" Afterward you can compare this with Ross Perot's argument that Mexicans are "too poor" to pay for American goods. All the common antitrade fallacies, from both sides of the border, can be answered by this venerable little Ricardian example. You can tell students that the error comes from looking only at "first-order" differences--that one country is "bigger" than the other in both dimensions--instead of at the "second-order" difference--that within Mexico trucks are cheaper relative to computers than they are within the United States.

A couple of freshmen once raised their hands in perplexity. "Do we have to *barter*?" asked one. "Can't we just cooperate to make each other better off?" This was a nice illustration of the emotions that can obscure the workings of the invisible hand. For many people, "competition" leads to thinking that the game must be zero-sum.

QUESTIONS

1. Is complete specialization for both countries a necessary condition for gains from trade to be realized between the countries? Explain.

    [No, as long as each country moves its production toward the good in which it has a comparative advantage, "surplus" production may be generated that can be used to trade for the other good. Of course, there could be further gains from trade if each country pursued complete specialization.]

2. What determines the slope of a production possibilities curve?

    [The slope of the PPC represents the opportunity costs of producing one good over another. In general, the opportunity cost depends on the suitability of resources used in the production of each good. For a straight-line PPC, in which the opportunity costs are constant, the resources used in the production of the two goods are perfect substitutes.]

REFERENCES/FURTHER READING

Roberts, Russell D. The Choice: A Fable of Free Trade and Protectionism. Prentice Hall, 1994.

Stodder, Jim. "A Simple Experiment of Comparative Advantage." Classroom Expernomics (Spring 1994): 8-10.

APPENDICES TO EXPERIMENT 2

- Graphs of Mexico's and the United States' production possibilities curves
- Student worksheet

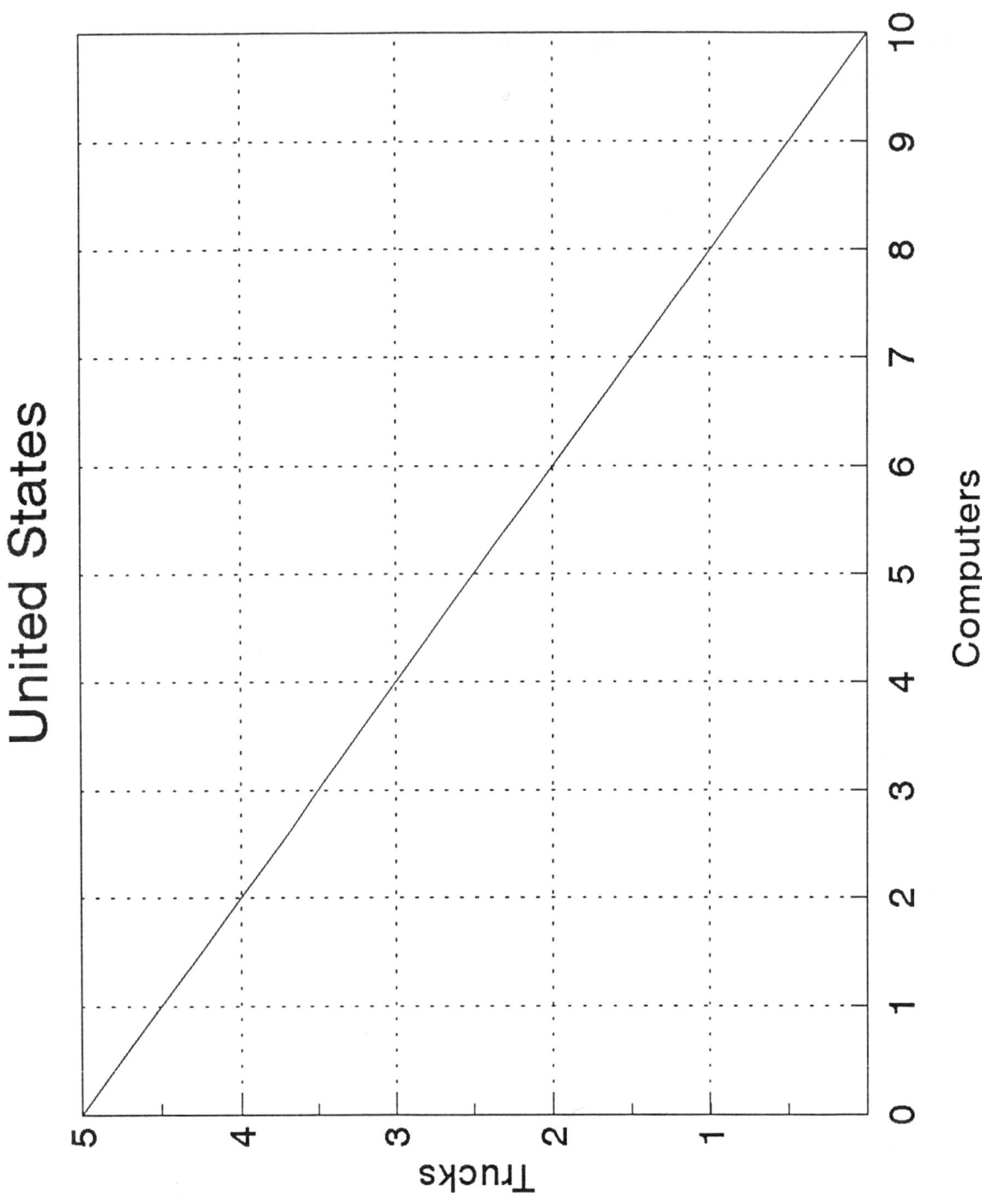

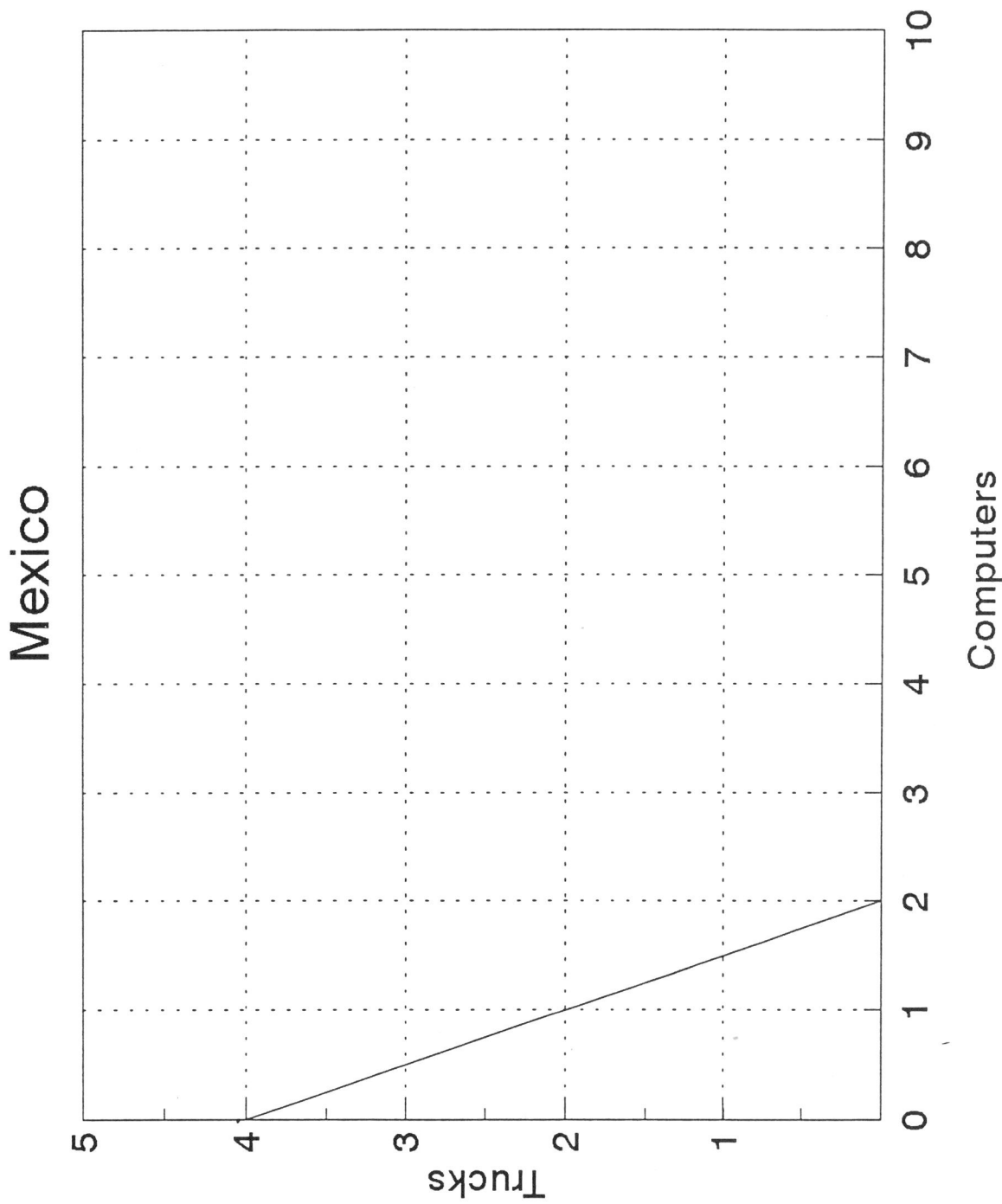

STUDENT WORKSHEET

1. The United States' initial "best point" represents _____ units of trucks and _____ units of computers.

2. Mexico's initial "best point" represents _____ units of trucks and _____ units of computers.

3. With respect to these best points, in which direction would each country have to move in order to become better off?

4. Now suppose that you can separate your country's consumption decision from its production decision. That is, suppose that you can now trade some of your production for some of the production of the other country. Describe a trade which would make both countries better off.

    The United States trades _____ units of _____ to Mexico for _____ units of _____.

    If each of you agree to this trade, please sign below to indicate your cooperation.

    _____   _____

5. What combination of trucks and computers does the United States produce after trade is allowed?

    _____ trucks and _____ computers

    What combination of trucks and computers does the United States consume after trade is allowed?

    _____ trucks and _____ computers

6. What combination of trucks and computers does Mexico produce after trade is allowed?

    _____ trucks and _____ computers

    What combination of trucks and computers does Mexico consume after trade is allowed?

    _____ trucks and _____ computers

EXPERIMENT 3: THE EXPERIMENTAL DERIVATION OF A MARKET DEMAND CURVE

OVERVIEW

This brief exercise takes very little time or effort, but provides a nice foundation for the discussion of market demand.[1] Like most simple classroom experiments, it allows students to use their own classroom experience to better understand an abstract economic concept--in this case, the demand curve. This exercise can be used to introduce or illustrate the law of demand, the use of the *ceteris paribus* assumption, and the effects of changes in the nonprice determinants of demand.

MATERIALS NEEDED

- Two cans of Coca-Cola (or other commodity of your choice)

ADMINISTERING THE EXPERIMENT

For the first lecture on demand, take two cans of Coke to class. Proceed by asking for a show of hands in response to each of the following questions.

1. How many of you are longing for an ice-cold Coke?

A positive response to this question reflects the *desire* to have a Coke. But desire alone does not constitute demand.

2. How many of you have money with you to buy a Coke?

A positive response to this question indicates the *ability* to buy a Coke. But ability alone does not constitute demand.

Tell the class that you will be selling the two cans of Coke to the two students who are willing to pay the most for them. Be certain that they understand that money (and the cans of Coke) will actually be changing hands. Then proceed with the following questions.

3. How many of you are willing to buy a Coke for ten cents?

---

[1] This is an edited version of an experiment that John Brock contributed to the Fall, 1992, issue of *Classroom Expernomics*.

At this point, begin to construct a table on the blackboard indicating the number of Cokes demanded at various prices and fill in the first line to record the quantity of Cokes demanded at a price of ten cents.

> 4. How many of you are willing to buy a Coke for twenty cents? ...For thirty cents? ...For forty cents? [Continue until only two hands are raised.]

Record the quantity demanded at each price in the table on the board, creating a demand schedule.

Now connect the data points to approximate the market demand curve. Or, if you prefer, create a "line of best fit" and explain how economists use regression analysis to estimate real-world demand relationships. This empirically derived market demand curve provides the foundation for a discussion of the law of demand, nonprice determinants of demand (in this case, the size of the class, the time of day that the class is held, the temperature, the price and availability of substitutes), and how changes in these nonprice determinants can shift the demand curve.

DISCUSSION

This "Coke game" is designed to bring to life a number of abstract economic concepts so that students will better understand and retain these important principles. The active nature of the game provides a welcome variation from the usual lecture format. Since actual trades (that is, money for Coke) take place, this experiment works especially well with relatively small classes.

QUESTIONS

> 1. Suppose that, due to a heating (cooling) system malfunction, the temperature inside the classroom was ten degrees warmer (cooler). What effect would this be likely to have on the position of the demand curve?
>
> [If the temperature were ten degrees warmer (cooler), there would probably be a larger (smaller) number of cans of Coke demanded at any price.]
>
> 2. Suppose that this exercise had been conducted in a class that was identical to this one, except that it was twice as large. What effect would this be likely to have on the position of the demand curve?
>
> [The quantity demanded of a commodity at any price varies positively with the market population. Hence, with a larger class, the demand curve would lie further to the right (*ceteris paribus*). If everything except size was identical between the two classes, including tastes, income, etc., then twice as much Coke should be demanded at each price.]

REFERENCES/FURTHER READING

Brock, John R. "Experimental Derivation of a Demand Curve." Classroom Expernomics (Fall 1992): 3-4.

Weidenaar, Dennis. "A Classroom Experiment Demonstrating the Generation of a Market Demand Function and the Determination of Equilibrium Price." Journal of Economic Education (Spring 1972): 94-100.

EXPERIMENT 4: THE DOUBLE ORAL AUCTION

OVERVIEW

The double oral auction is perhaps the best known of all classroom "experiments." As demonstrated in Chapter 7 of Taylor's *Economics*, the double oral auction serves as both a powerful illustration of the market at work and as strong evidence that the competitive equilibrium works well in predicting actual market outcomes (under conditions much less strict than those that are generally attributed to a perfectly competitive market, we might add). Originally the object of the experimental research of Vernon Smith, the results of this auction have proven to be quite robust, making it ideal for classroom use. The double oral auction is also notable for its versatility. It can be used to illustrate the impact of the implementation of price controls or the imposition of taxes (also discussed in Chapter 7 of *Economics*). By imposing price controls, market shortages and surpluses can be induced and the winners and losers can be identified. The impact of a tax on equilibrium price and quantity and the level of revenue generated can be directly observed in these markets, providing a basis for the discussion of the concepts of economic efficiency (that is, the deadweight loss of a tax) and the incidence of a tax.

Here, we describe a basic double oral auction experiment similar to the one presented in Taylor's text, but with different marginal cost and marginal benefit data. Instructions for several variations involving the implementation of taxes appear in Experiment 5.

For those instructors who have access to a networked computer laboratory, two computerized versions of the double auction are currently available.[1]

MATERIALS NEEDED

- A large blackboard or other writing surface for the recording of bids, asks, and transactions
- Buyers' and sellers' record sheets containing marginal benefit and marginal cost schedules to distribute to the market participants

---

[1] The University of Arizona has developed a program called ESLDA (Economic Science Laboratory Double Auction) and the California Institute of Technology has developed a program called MUDA (Multiple Unit Double Auction). For details on procuring a copy of ESLDA, contact Shawn LaMaster, Economic Science Laboratory, University of Arizona, Tucson, AZ 85721. For more information on MUDA, contact Charles Plott, Department of Economics and Political Science, California Institute of Technology, Pasadena, CA 91125.

ADMINISTERING THE EXPERIMENT

Students participate in a market as buyers and/or sellers of an unspecified product.[2] Equal numbers of students are designated to participate as buyers and sellers.[3] The buyers' record sheets are randomly distributed to the buyers, and the sellers' record sheets are randomly distributed to the sellers. Each buyer's record sheet includes a buyer ID (for example, "Buyer #2") and the marginal benefit that accrues to that buyer when each consecutive unit of the product is purchased during any single trading period. Similarly, each seller's record sheet includes a seller ID and the marginal cost that a particular seller incurs when each consecutive unit of the product is produced and sold during any single trading period.[4] These record sheets also provide space in which a buyer or seller can record the price and the net benefit (that is, the marginal benefit minus the purchase price for buyers; the selling price minus the marginal cost for sellers) of each unit bought or sold.

A trading period opens with an announcement that "the market for trading period x is now open." Communication between buyers and sellers is limited to the announcement of bids and asks.[5] The communication of their private marginal benefit and marginal cost information to other traders is strictly prohibited. Buyers make bids and sellers communicate asks using statements of the following form:

Bids (buyers): "Buyer number n bids $xx for one unit."
Asks (sellers): " Seller number n asks $xx for one unit."

Bids and asks are recorded on the blackboard (in sight of all market participants) by the market manager.[6] For example, suppose that seller #4 asks $10 for one unit; the market manager immediately posts that offer on the blackboard. If buyer #1 then bids $5, that bid would also be posted immediately and the blackboard would look like this:[7]

---

[2] When the product being traded in the market is unspecified, students do not bring to the market any preconceived notion of the "appropriate" price at which to buy or sell it.

[3] Issues of class size, how many students to have participate, whether to have students participate individually or as teams, etc., are addressed in the Discussion section that follows.

[4] A particular unit is produced only if the seller successfully enters into a contract to sell that unit; hence, the marginal cost of any particular unit is incurred only when that unit is sold.

[5] Asks are also frequently called "offers" in the double oral auction literature.

[6] The role of market manager (sometimes known as the "pit boss") is almost always played by the instructor.

[7] Some experienced instructors prefer to record only completed transactions (that is, the price and the buyer and seller IDs) since this significantly reduces the amount of time required to complete a trading period and hence increases the number of trading periods that can be run in a single class. If all asks and bids are recorded, we find it useful to record them in the format shown above because it makes the recording of data a bit more compact. This is a minor point, perhaps, but one that will be appreciated by anyone who has moved back and forth frenetically from the bid to the ask column as buyers and sellers have shouted out bids and asks in rapid succession.

ACCEPTED BY	BID	BUYER #	SELLER #	ASK	ACCEPTED BY
	5.00	1	4	10.00	

Once a bid or ask is announced and recorded, any new bid must be higher than the last posted bid and any new ask must be lower than the last posted ask. New bids and asks are posted immediately below the previous entries.

A transaction takes place when a buyer accepts an existing ask or when a seller accepts an existing bid. At this point, the transaction (including the buyer ID, the seller ID, and the price) is recorded for future reference.[8]

After a transaction is made and recorded, the trading period continues.[9] All outstanding bids and offers are erased, and the bid/ask process begins again. New bids and asks are posted as they occur, and a transaction is made whenever a current bid or ask is accepted. The trading period can end in one of two ways. Some instructors utilize a "hard close"; that is, they set the duration of the trading period in advance and close the market when the specified time period expires. This method has two advantages: 1) placing a time limit on participants may speed up the bid/ask/acceptance process, and 2) fixing the length of trading periods simplifies planning, since the amount of time that it will take to run a market for a given number of periods can be predicted almost exactly. Other instructors prefer to end a trading period using a "soft close" in which the pace of bids, offers, and acceptances eventually slows down and finally grinds to a halt. At this point, buyers and sellers are given a final opportunity to accept the most recent ask and bid. If none is forthcoming, it is announced that "the market for trading period x is now closed." The advantage of the soft close is that it eliminates the risk that a trading period may be terminated before some mutually beneficial transactions have been made (as sometimes happens during the initial trading period or two when buyers and sellers are still somewhat hesitant) and may thus encourage more rapid convergence toward the competitive equilibrium during the initial trading period(s).

At this point, students can be given a minute to compute their net gains for the market period. The market is then opened for the next trading period. Trading proceeds as just described until new bids and offers cease, at which point the market for that trading period is closed. Any additional periods proceed in the same manner.

Prices and quantities transacted will usually converge to something very close to the competitive equilibrium price and quantity within a few periods. At this point, the market exercise can be analyzed in terms of the relevant economic theories. The individual buyers' demand curves consist of a series of downward-sloping steps, and their horizontal summation yields the market demand curve, which is also in the form of a downward-sloping step function.

---

[8]If blackboard space is plentiful, simply post the ID of the accepting buyer or seller and circle the transaction data; otherwise, record it elsewhere on the board, erase all previous bids and asks, and begin the process again.

[9]After the first transaction or two, it may be useful to remind the buyer and seller involved in the transaction that they have bought/sold their first units and should now consider the marginal values for their *second* units in making subsequent bids/offers; other buyers and sellers should still consider the marginal values for their *first* units.

Double Oral Auction

The individual sellers' supply curves (that is, their marginal cost curves) consist of a series of upward-sloping steps, and their horizontal summation yields the market supply curve, which takes the form of an upward-sloping step function. The intersection of the market supply and demand curves yields predictions of the price and the number of units traded. These predictions will almost always be quite close to the results that have been observed in the double oral auction demonstration market. The market supply and demand curves in Figure 1 are derived from the marginal benefit and marginal cost data that appear in the record sheets found in the Appendices at the end of this experiment. For these values, the competitive equilibrium model predicts that 8 units will be traded in each trading period at prices between $21 and $22.

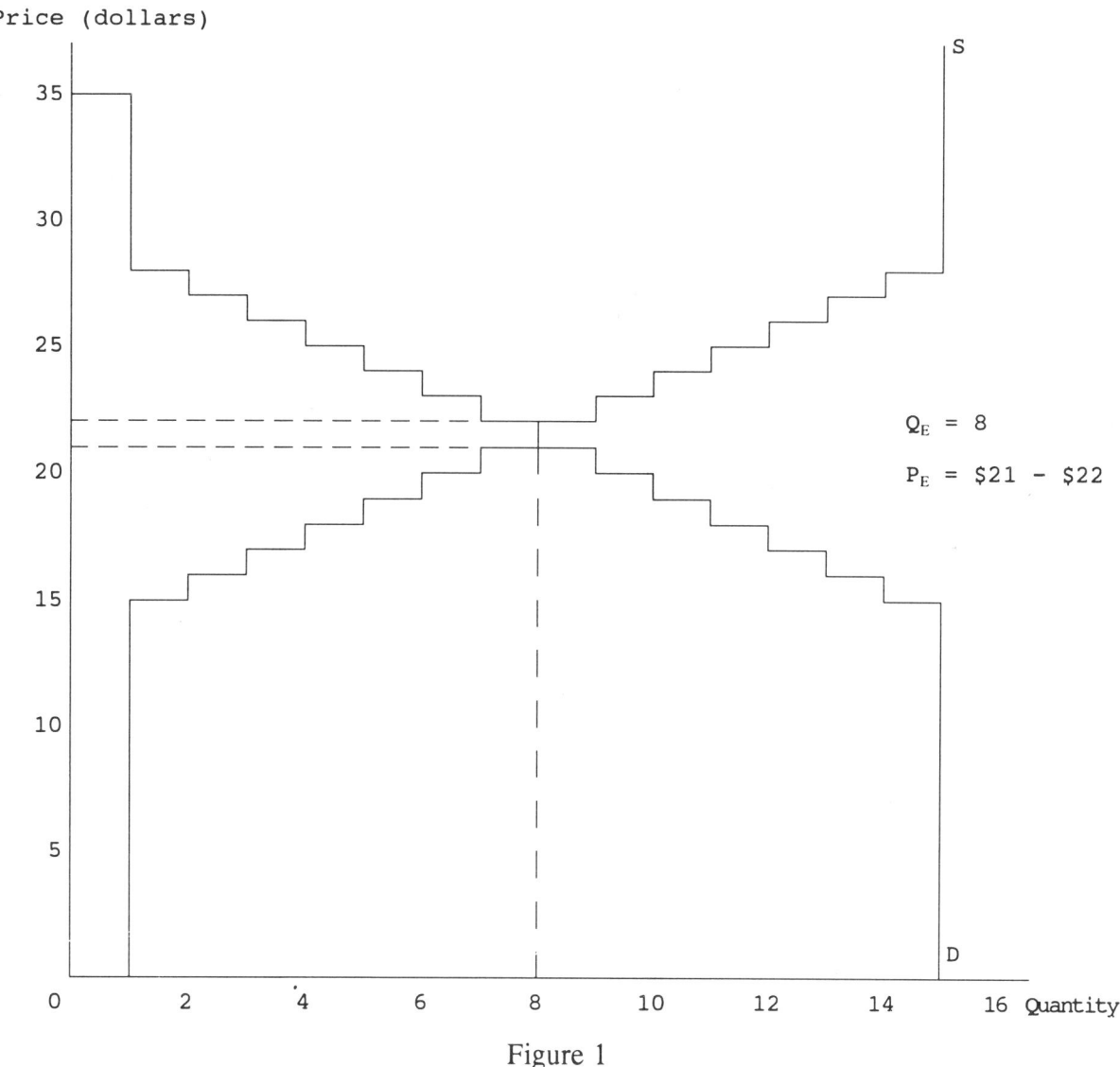

Figure 1

Several schemes exist for comparing the results of the demonstration market with the equilibrium predictions. The simplest and least time-consuming is simply to compare the quantity traded and the average price in each period of the demonstration market with the equilibrium quantity and price. The quantity traded will usually converge to the equilibrium quantity quickly, and the average price will usually converge toward the equilibrium price in each consecutive period. A somewhat more time-consuming alternative is to plot the prices of each unit traded in each period against the equilibrium price. Suppose, for example, that 7 units were sold during the first trading period, and 8 units were traded during the second trading period. Further suppose that the trades were made at the following prices: $24, $23, $19, $22, $20, $22, and $21 during the first trading period, and $22, $19, $19, $22, $20, $22, $22, and $21 during the second trading period. The results for these two periods would be presented as in Figure 2.

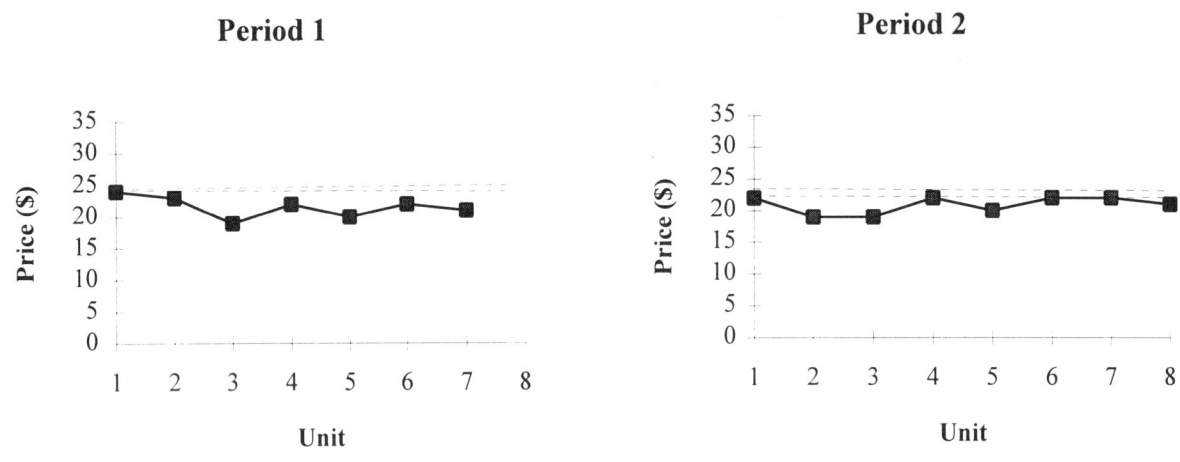

Figure 2

DISCUSSION

We can think of no better way to illustrate the power of Adam Smith's "invisible hand" than by having students participate in a double oral auction experiment. At the beginning of this market exercise, students are often convinced that their "strategy" will be an important determinant of their net benefits. By the end of the exercise, however, students usually realize just how powerless they are to affect the market. To quote Chapter 7 of the textbook, "When one watches such a market, one can almost see the invisible hand working." We would add that when one participates in such a market, one can actually <u>feel</u> the invisible hand working. This experiment should convince students that the competitive equilibrium model is a powerful predictor of market behavior under at least some market conditions. This result is even more impressive when one considers that two of the conditions that are traditionally cited as requirements for a perfectly competitive market are absent. The number of buyers and sellers who participate in classroom versions of the double oral auction is usually quite small,[10] and

---

[10]Convergence toward the competitive equilibrium regularly occurs with as few as eight market participants (four buyers and four sellers).

each of these participants possesses only a small amount of purely private information. Nevertheless, the double auction rarely fails to converge to the competitive equilibrium within a few trading periods.

There are several practical issues that must be addressed by anyone who is contemplating running a double auction in the classroom. The first is the question of how many market participants to involve. We have provided five buyers' record sheets and five sellers' record sheets in the Appendices at the end of this experiment. This allows an instructor with a class of ten to involve *all* students fully in this market exercise. Of course, a principles class with only ten students would be something of a rarity at most institutions. With larger class sizes, several options exist, each with its own set of advantages and disadvantages.

One option is to have ten students participate in the market while other students in the class observe. Since the number of buyers and sellers participating in the market exercise is certain, so are the equilibrium price and quantity. On the other hand, there is little doubt that this exercise is most beneficial to those students who participate rather than merely observe. So its impact is likely to be diminished if only a subset of the students in the class actually participates.[11]

Several options are available if one wishes to involve larger numbers of students in the exercise. One possibility is to fill the role of each buyer and seller with a team of students who jointly make decisions to bid or ask. However, if bids and asks are formulated jointly, the experiment will probably proceed a bit more tentatively, and this may hinder convergence to the equilibrium. This problem can be reduced or eliminated by having individual team members make decisions on behalf of the entire team in alternate trading periods.

Another possibility is to assign each set of marginal benefit and cost data to two (or more) students. In this way, one can quickly create a market exercise that will directly involve twenty (or thirty) students rather than ten.[12] If this is done, the equilibrium price prediction remains unchanged, while the equilibrium quantity will double (or triple). Since the length of time needed to complete a trading period varies directly with the number of units traded, this option will increase the amount of time necessary to complete the exercise.

Once you have a bit of experience conducting this market exercise, it is easy to customize a version that will generate any desired equilibrium price and quantity for any desired number of participants. We offer the following bit of advice to those of you who design your own

---

[11]However, for instructors of very large classes, having a subset of the class participate may be the only practical option.

[12]Of course, there is no reason why the number of students participating can't be some number *between* ten and twenty, or *between* twenty and thirty. Nor is it necessary that the number of buyers and sellers be exactly equal. But if, say, twenty-three marginal benefit and marginal cost schedules are passed out from a set of thirty that were taken to class, it will be almost impossible to know the equilibrium price and quantity without determining exactly *which* marginal cost and marginal benefit schedules were passed out and constructing the market demand and supply schedules.

experiments. Always assign marginal benefits and costs so that each market participant will be able to buy or sell at least *one* unit per period. In some versions of this exercise, each market participant is given a single unit that he or she can attempt to buy or sell per market period, but not all of these units will be traded in the competitive equilibrium. In this situation, buyers whose marginal benefits are "too low" and sellers whose marginal costs are "too high" quickly learn that they cannot successfully participate in the market and tend to lose interest in the exercise. At a minimum, each participant should have at least two units he or she can attempt to buy or sell, and the marginal benefit and cost values should be assigned such that each market participant will be able to buy or sell at least one unit per period in equilibrium.[13]

A word is in order concerning the use of bonus points (or any other rewards) to motivate students in this exercise.[14] Since the net benefit attainable by buyers or sellers depends on the particular marginal benefit or marginal cost values that they are assigned, many instructors allocate bonus points based on the *proportion* of the expected consumer surplus--that is, $(MB - P)/(MB - P_E)$ for each unit purchased--attained by buyers and the *proportion* of the expected producer surplus--that is, $(P - MC)/(P_E - P)$ for each unit sold--attained by sellers. If you use this method, it is important that you assign marginal costs and marginal benefits symmetrically around the equilibrium price. Otherwise, you may induce a pattern of convergence toward the equilibrium price that gives certain participants an unfair advantage over others in the market.

There is one rather subtle difference between the competitive equilibrium illustrated in this manual and that described in Figure 7.5 in the textbook. In each case, since both the market demand and the market supply curves consist of a series of steps, their intersection occurs not at a single point but over a vertical or a horizontal segment of the curves. In Figure 7.5 in the textbook, the market demand and supply curves intersect over a horizontal segment of each curve between the quantities of 12 and 13. As a practical matter, this means that if the thirteenth unit is traded, neither the buyer nor the seller will realize a net benefit (or a net loss). This makes the equilibrium quantity indeterminate (and the equilibrium price determinate). The marginal benefit and cost data used to generate Figure 1 in this manual yields market supply and demand curves that intersect over a vertical portion of the curves. This means that the equilibrium quantity is determinate, while there is a range of equilibrium prices. We prefer the latter situation because it allows the equilibrium quantity to be predicted with precision, and the

---

[13] In order to keep track of what the equilibrium quantity will be when you are not certain how many students will attend the class, construct the individual marginal benefit and cost schedules such that each buyer and each seller will be able to trade exactly *one* unit. This can be accomplished by assigning marginal costs such that each seller's first unit has a marginal cost less than the equilibrium price, while any additional units have marginal costs above the equilibrium price. Assign marginal benefits so that each buyer's first unit has a marginal benefit greater than the equilibrium price, while any additional units have marginal benefits less than the equilibrium price. By assigning equal numbers of students to be buyers and sellers, you can ensure that the equilibrium quantity will be equal to the number of buyers (or sellers) in the market. In the event that an odd number of students appear in the class, simply draft one student to record the transactions.

[14] Even in the absence of such rewards, the natural competitiveness of most students will lead these markets to converge toward the competitive equilibrium.

prediction will usually correctly predict the number of units traded in the market exercise.[15] The observed price, on the other hand, will usually converge toward the equilibrium price, but seldom will all transactions take place at exactly the equilibrium price. So prices are more likely to conform to the competitive equilibrium prediction if the latter encompasses a range of prices.[16]

There is also a small difference in the pattern of marginal benefit and marginal cost values that we have assigned to buyers and sellers. Note that the first unit purchased by one of the buyers has been assigned a rather extreme marginal benefit, while the first unit sold by one of the sellers has been assigned an extreme marginal cost. Our motivation for assigning these extreme values will become apparent in the questions that follow.

Finally, once you have acquired a bit of confidence that the market exercise will actually generate something near the competitive equilibrium prediction, an impressive bit of showmanship becomes possible. Simply announce to the class that you are going to write down your prediction of how many units will be traded during each trading period and the range of prices at which trades will take place, seal your prediction in an envelope, and give it to one of your students before beginning the market exercise. At the end of the exercise, ask the student to open the envelope and announce your prediction to the class. Students will almost certainly leave the exercise impressed with your predictive powers.

QUESTIONS

1. (To sellers) What do you believe was the *highest* marginal benefit to any buyer from the purchase of a unit?

   (To buyers) What do you believe was the *lowest* marginal cost to any seller of producing a unit?

   [Sellers usually speculate that the highest marginal benefit was around the highest bid they observed during the market exercise. They are often surprised to learn that the highest marginal benefit was much higher than the highest bid they observed. But any buyer with an unusually high marginal benefit has no reason to reveal it.]

   [Buyers usually speculate that the lowest marginal cost was around the value of the lowest ask they observed during the exercise. But any seller with an unusually low marginal cost has no reason to reveal it. So buyers are frequently quite surprised to learn that one unit could be produced at a marginal cost of zero.]

---

[15]That is, it will be correct unless market participants either fail to make beneficial trades or make trades that are not beneficial.

[16]Although it is still reasonably likely that not all units will be traded at prices within the range of equilibrium prices, many of them will be. And the average price at which units are traded will almost certainly be within or very near the equilibrium range.

2. What would be the effect of imposing a $4 per unit tax on sellers for each unit sold? What would be the effect of imposing a $4 per unit tax on buyers for each unit purchased?

[Both taxes would reduce the equilibrium quantity in this market from 8 to 6 units. Hence, the deadweight loss of the tax would be the same in each case. If the tax were imposed on sellers, the equilibrium price would rise from the $21-$22 range to the $23-$24 range (that is, sellers would be able to pass on approximately half of the tax to buyers). If the tax were imposed on buyers, the equilibrium price would fall to the $19-$20 range (that is, buyers would be able to shift approximately half of the tax to sellers). Hence, the incidence of the tax would be the same in each case. To demonstrate this result experimentally, see Experiment 5.]

REFERENCES/FURTHER READING

Smith, Vernon L. "An Experimental Study of Competitive Market Behavior." Journal of Political Economy (April 1962): 111-137.

_____. "Markets as Economizers of Information: Experimental Examination of the 'Hayek Hypothesis.'" Economic Inquiry (April 1982): 165-179.

APPENDICES TO EXPERIMENT 4

- Instructions for participants in the double oral auction experiment
- Buyers' record sheets to be distributed to those students who are assigned to the role of buyers
- Sellers' record sheets to be distributed to those students who have been assigned to the role of sellers

The instructions may be distributed to all members of the class, or they may simply be read aloud prior to commencing the first trading period (but after the buyers' and sellers' record sheets have been distributed).

STUDENT INSTRUCTIONS

You are about to participate in a market exercise known as a double oral auction. You (and each of the other students who are participating) have been assigned to the role of either buyer or seller. If you are a seller, you have been assigned a "seller ID" number, which appears on the seller's record sheet that accompanies these instructions. If you are buyer, you have been assigned a "buyer ID" number on the buyer's record sheet that accompanies these instructions. With the exception of your buyer or seller ID number, the information on these sheets is purely private, and you are not to share it with anyone.

This market will operate over a number of "trading periods." If you are a seller, you may make available for sale up to three units during each trading period. Each time that you sell a unit, you incur the marginal cost that is associated with that unit on your seller's record sheet. If you are a buyer, you may buy up to three units during each trading period. Each time you buy a unit, you realize the marginal benefit that is associated with that unit on your buyer's record sheet. Your goal is to maximize your net benefit from selling or buying these units. You need not trade any unit unless you realize a net benefit.

When a trading period opens, sellers and buyers announce the prices at which they are willing to trade a single unit by calling out asks or bids in the following form:

Asks (sellers): "Seller number *n* asks $*xx* for one unit."
Bids (buyers): "Buyer number *n* bids $*xx* for one unit."

Bids and asks are recorded on the blackboard (in sight of all market participants) by the market manager. Once a bid or ask is announced, any new bid must be higher than the previous bid and any new ask must be lower than the previous ask. A unit is traded when a buyer accepts an existing ask (by calling out "Buyer number *n* accepts") or when a seller accepts an existing bid (by calling out "Seller number *n* accepts"). At this point, the buyer and seller involved in the transaction should record the selling/purchase price on their record sheets and calculate their net benefit from the transaction. The transaction will also be recorded by the market manager for future reference. Once a buyer or seller has sold a particular unit in a trading period, that unit is no longer available for trading, and buyers and sellers should refer to the marginal cost/benefit of their next unit in making subsequent asks or bids during the remainder of the trading period.

After the transaction is recorded, the trading period will continue. The bid/ask/acceptance process will begin again. When bids, asks, and acceptances cease, the market will be closed for the period.

During subsequent trading periods, trading will proceed in the same manner. At the beginning of each trading period, each buyer and seller again has three units to trade, regardless of the number of units he or she was able to trade during the previous period. The number of trading periods will be determined by the market manager.

Remember that as an individual buyer or seller, your goal is to realize the largest possible net benefit over the course of the exercise. This can be accomplished by maximizing the net benefit on each unit that you buy or sell.

BUYERS' RECORD SHEETS

BUYER #1   NAME _____

UNIT BOUGHT	TRADING PERIOD:	1	2	3	4
1	MARGINAL BENEFIT	$28	$28	$28	$28
	PURCHASE PRICE	___	___	___	___
	NET BENEFIT	___	___	___	___
2	MARGINAL BENEFIT	$22	$22	$22	$22
	PURCHASE PRICE	___	___	___	___
	NET BENEFIT	___	___	___	___
3	MARGINAL BENEFIT	$17	$17	$17	$17
	PURCHASE PRICE	___	___	___	___
	NET BENEFIT	___	___	___	___

NET BENEFIT (ALL UNITS) ___   ___   ___   ___

NET BENEFIT (ALL PERIODS)   ___

BUYER #2   NAME _____

UNIT BOUGHT	TRADING PERIOD:	1	2	3	4
1	MARGINAL BENEFIT	$35	$35	$35	$35
	PURCHASE PRICE	___	___	___	___
	NET BENEFIT	___	___	___	___
2	MARGINAL BENEFIT	$20	$20	$20	$20
	PURCHASE PRICE	___	___	___	___
	NET BENEFIT	___	___	___	___
3	MARGINAL BENEFIT	$18	$18	$18	$18
	PURCHASE PRICE	___	___	___	___
	NET BENEFIT	___	___	___	___

NET BENEFIT (ALL UNITS) ___   ___   ___   ___

NET BENEFIT (ALL PERIODS)   ___

Double Oral Auction

```
BUYER #3                                     NAME _____

UNIT
BOUGHT  TRADING PERIOD:      1         2         3         4
-----------------------------------------------------------------------
        MARGINAL BENEFIT    $27       $27       $27       $27

  1     PURCHASE PRICE     _____     _____     _____     _____

        NET BENEFIT        _____     _____     _____     _____
-----------------------------------------------------------------------
        MARGINAL BENEFIT    $21       $21       $21       $21

  2     PURCHASE PRICE     _____     _____     _____     _____

        NET BENEFIT        _____     _____     _____     _____
-----------------------------------------------------------------------
        MARGINAL BENEFIT    $15       $15       $15       $15

  3     PURCHASE PRICE     _____     _____     _____     _____

        NET BENEFIT        _____     _____     _____     _____
-----------------------------------------------------------------------

        NET BENEFIT (ALL UNITS)   _____    _____    _____    _____

        NET BENEFIT (ALL PERIODS)                             _____
```

```
BUYER #4                                     NAME _____

UNIT
BOUGHT  TRADING PERIOD:      1         2         3         4
-----------------------------------------------------------------------
        MARGINAL BENEFIT    $25       $25       $25       $25

  1     PURCHASE PRICE     _____     _____     _____     _____

        NET BENEFIT        _____     _____     _____     _____
-----------------------------------------------------------------------
        MARGINAL BENEFIT    $24       $24       $24       $24

  2     PURCHASE PRICE     _____     _____     _____     _____

        NET BENEFIT        _____     _____     _____     _____
-----------------------------------------------------------------------
        MARGINAL BENEFIT    $19       $19       $19       $19

  3     PURCHASE PRICE     _____     _____     _____     _____

        NET BENEFIT        _____     _____     _____     _____
-----------------------------------------------------------------------

        NET BENEFIT (ALL UNITS)   _____    _____    _____    _____

        NET BENEFIT (ALL PERIODS)                             _____
```

BUYER #5   NAME _____

UNIT BOUGHT	TRADING PERIOD:	1	2	3	4
1	MARGINAL BENEFIT	$26	$26	$26	$26
	PURCHASE PRICE	____	____	____	____
	NET BENEFIT	____	____	____	____
2	MARGINAL BENEFIT	$23	$23	$23	$23
	PURCHASE PRICE	____	____	____	____
	NET BENEFIT	____	____	____	____
3	MARGINAL BENEFIT	$16	$16	$16	$16
	PURCHASE PRICE	____	____	____	____
	NET BENEFIT	____	____	____	____
	NET BENEFIT (ALL UNITS)	____	____	____	____
	NET BENEFIT (ALL PERIODS)				____

SELLERS' RECORD SHEETS

SELLER #1   NAME _____

UNIT SOLD	TRADING PERIOD:	1	2	3	4
1	SELLING PRICE	____	____	____	____
	MARGINAL COST	$18	$18	$18	$18
	NET BENEFIT	____	____	____	____
2	SELLING PRICE	____	____	____	____
	MARGINAL COST	$22	$22	$22	$22
	NET BENEFIT	____	____	____	____
3	SELLING PRICE	____	____	____	____
	MARGINAL COST	$24	$24	$24	$24
	NET BENEFIT	____	____	____	____
	NET BENEFIT (ALL UNITS)	____	____	____	____
	NET BENEFIT (ALL PERIODS)				____

Double Oral Auction 35

SELLER #2   NAME _____

UNIT SOLD	TRADING PERIOD:	1	2	3	4
1	SELLING PRICE	___	___	___	___
	MARGINAL COST	$16	$16	$16	$16
	NET BENEFIT	___	___	___	___
2	SELLING PRICE	___	___	___	___
	MARGINAL COST	$21	$21	$21	$21
	NET BENEFIT	___	___	___	___
3	SELLING PRICE	___	___	___	___
	MARGINAL COST	$25	$25	$25	$25
	NET BENEFIT	___	___	___	___

NET BENEFIT (ALL UNITS) ___ ___ ___ ___

NET BENEFIT (ALL PERIODS) ___

SELLER #3   NAME _____

UNIT SOLD	TRADING PERIOD:	1	2	3	4
1	SELLING PRICE	___	___	___	___
	MARGINAL COST	$ 0	$ 0	$ 0	$ 0
	NET BENEFIT	___	___	___	___
2	SELLING PRICE	___	___	___	___
	MARGINAL COST	$19	$19	$19	$19
	NET BENEFIT	___	___	___	___
3	SELLING PRICE	___	___	___	___
	MARGINAL COST	$26	$26	$26	$26
	NET BENEFIT	___	___	___	___

NET BENEFIT (ALL UNITS) ___ ___ ___ ___

NET BENEFIT (ALL PERIODS) ___

Experiment 4

SELLER #4   NAME _____

UNIT SOLD	TRADING PERIOD:	1	2	3	4
1	SELLING PRICE	____	____	____	____
	MARGINAL COST	$15	$15	$15	$15
	NET BENEFIT	____	____	____	____
2	SELLING PRICE	____	____	____	____
	MARGINAL COST	$23	$23	$23	$23
	NET BENEFIT	____	____	____	____
3	SELLING PRICE	____	____	____	____
	MARGINAL COST	$28	$28	$28	$28
	NET BENEFIT	____	____	____	____

NET BENEFIT (ALL UNITS) ____   ____   ____   ____

NET BENEFIT (ALL PERIODS)   ____

SELLER #5   NAME _____

UNIT SOLD	TRADING PERIOD:	1	2	3	4
1	SELLING PRICE	____	____	____	____
	MARGINAL COST	$17	$17	$17	$17
	NET BENEFIT	____	____	____	____
2	SELLING PRICE	____	____	____	____
	MARGINAL COST	$20	$20	$20	$20
	NET BENEFIT	____	____	____	____
3	SELLING PRICE	____	____	____	____
	MARGINAL COST	$27	$27	$27	$27
	NET BENEFIT	____	____	____	____

NET BENEFIT (ALL UNITS) ____   ____   ____   ____

NET BENEFIT (ALL PERIODS)   ____

EXPERIMENT 5: THE DOUBLE ORAL AUCTION WITH PRICE CONTROLS/TAXES

OVERVIEW

Once the predictive ability of the competitive equilibrium model has been established experimentally (see Experiment 4) and the efficiency of the competitive equilibrium has been established, the double oral auction can be used to examine the welfare effects of various forms of market intervention by the government. Two common forms of market intervention involve the imposition of price controls and the implementation of taxes. By comparing the percentage of potential consumer and producer surplus achieved in the double oral auction when price controls or taxes are present with the percentage of surplus achieved in the basic double oral auction experiment, it is possible to observe the deadweight loss that results from the government intervention in the market.[1] This experiment contains several variations that involve the imposition of either price controls or a specific tax. In the tax variation, the experiment also provides a basis for a discussion of tax incidence and the importance of supply and demand elasticities in its determination.

MATERIALS NEEDED

- A large blackboard or other writing surface for the recording of bids, asks, and transactions
- Buyers' and sellers' record sheets containing marginal benefit and marginal cost schedules to distribute to the market participants

ADMINISTERING THE EXPERIMENT

The experiment proceeds in the same manner as the basic double oral auction experiment described in Experiment 4. The following procedures are therefore presented in a somewhat abbreviated form. For a more thorough discussion, see Experiment 4. If you have already run the basic double oral auction experiment, proceed directly to variation 1 (to examine the effects of price controls) or variation 2 (to examine the effects of a specific tax), using the same marginal benefit and cost data you used in the basic double oral auction experiment. If you have not yet conducted the basic double oral auction, we provide the following abbreviated set of procedures for doing so before you proceed to variation 1 or 2.

Equal numbers of students participate as buyers and sellers of an unspecified product. Each buyer's record sheet includes a buyer ID and the marginal benefit that accrues to that buyer when each consecutive unit of the product is purchased during a single trading period. Each seller's record sheet includes a seller ID and the marginal cost that a particular seller incurs

---

[1] All of this assumes the absence of externalities in the market.

when each consecutive unit of the product is produced and sold during a single trading period.

A trading period opens with the announcement that "the market for trading period x is now open." Communication between buyers and sellers is limited to the announcement of bids and asks. The communication of their private marginal benefit and marginal cost information to other traders is strictly prohibited. Buyers make bids and sellers communicate asks using statements of the following form:

> Bids (buyers): "Buyer number n bids $xx for one unit."
> Asks (sellers): "Seller number n asks $xx for one unit."

Bids and asks are recorded on the blackboard (in sight of all market participants) by the market manager. Once a bid or ask is announced and recorded, any new bid must be higher than the last posted bid, and any new ask must be lower than the last posted ask. New bids and asks are posted immediately below the previous entries.

A transaction takes place when a buyer accepts an existing ask or when a seller accepts an existing bid. At this point, the transaction (including the buyer ID, the seller ID, and the price) is recorded for future reference.

After a transaction is made and recorded, the trading period continues. All outstanding bids and offers are erased, and the bid/ask process begins again. New bids and asks are posted as they occur, and a transaction is made whenever a current bid or ask is accepted. Each trading period can end using either a "hard close" or a "soft close."[2]

Give students a minute to compute their net gains for the market period and to record them on their record sheets. Then open the market for the next trading period. Trading proceeds as just described until new bids and offers cease, at which point the market for the current trading period is closed. Proceed in this manner for several periods until prices and quantities transacted converge to something close to the competitive equilibrium price and quantity ($Q_E = 8$ and P_E between $21 and $22 for the record sheets contained in the Appendices that follow this experiment).[3] If you have already conducted the basic double oral auction, you can skip this first stage of the experiment and proceed directly to implement price controls (Variation 1) or a specific tax (Variation 2).

---

[2] For a description and discussion of the advantages and disadvantages of each type of close, please see Experiment 4.

[3] If you have already run the basic double oral auction experiment (that is, Experiment 4), this first stage of the current experiment may be omitted. Simply provide each buyer and seller with a new record sheet with a marginal benefit or marginal cost schedule identical to the one he or she used in the first experiment (if students have placed their names on and turned in their record sheets from the first experiment, this is easy to accomplish). Begin the second experiment by imposing the price control or the tax and compare the results with those generated by the first experiment.

The following discussion will proceed under the assumption that the basic double oral auction was conducted using the marginal benefit and cost values contained on the record sheets in the Appendices which follow. If you have used different marginal benefit and cost values, you will need to examine your data to determine what price ceiling and/or floor to impose in order to induce the desired reduction in equilibrium quantity.

Variation 1: Price Controls

Impose an effective price ceiling on the market by announcing to the class that, beginning with the next period, no transaction may be completed at any price above $20. With the price ceiling in effect, 6 units should be sold at a price at or approaching $20 (see Figure 1). Run the market for one or more periods until the quantity and price adjust to these levels. (You should see very rapid convergence in this case.) Compare (or have students compare) the total consumer and producer surplus (that is, the sum of all of their "net benefits") from the last period in which the market was run without price controls with the total consumer and producer surplus during the last period in which the market was run with the price ceiling. The difference is the deadweight loss that results from the imposition of the price ceiling. By examining the changes in their individual payoffs, students can also analyze who benefits and who is harmed by the price ceiling.

If time permits, eliminate the price ceiling and instead impose a price floor that should have an equal effect on the expected quantity transacted (for example, a price floor of $23 for our marginal benefit and marginal cost values) and run the market for one or more additional periods until the market approaches the expected market quantity and price (that is, six units at a price of $23). Again have students compare the total consumer and producer surplus in the last period run with the price floor with that attained during the last period run without price controls *and* with that attained during the last period run with the price ceiling. The deadweight loss generated by the price ceiling and that generated by the price floor should be nearly equal. But the benefits and losses will be allocated among the buyers and sellers in a much different fashion.

Variation 2: A Specific Tax

Inform the class that, beginning with the next period, sellers must pay a specific tax on each unit that they sell. If you use the marginal benefit and marginal cost schedules in the record sheets found at the end of this experiment, a $4 tax on sellers should result in a reduction in the equilibrium quantity from 8 to 6 units and an increase in the equilibrium price from $21-$22 to $23-$24 (see Figure 2). After announcing the tax, run the market for several additional periods, until prices and quantities transacted converge to something resembling the new equilibrium.[4]

---

[4] If you are so inclined (and if time permits), eliminate the tax on sellers and impose it on buyers instead and run the market for several additional periods. The equilibrium quantity should converge to the same level while the equilibrium price should be in the range of $19-$20.

Price (dollars)

Figure 1

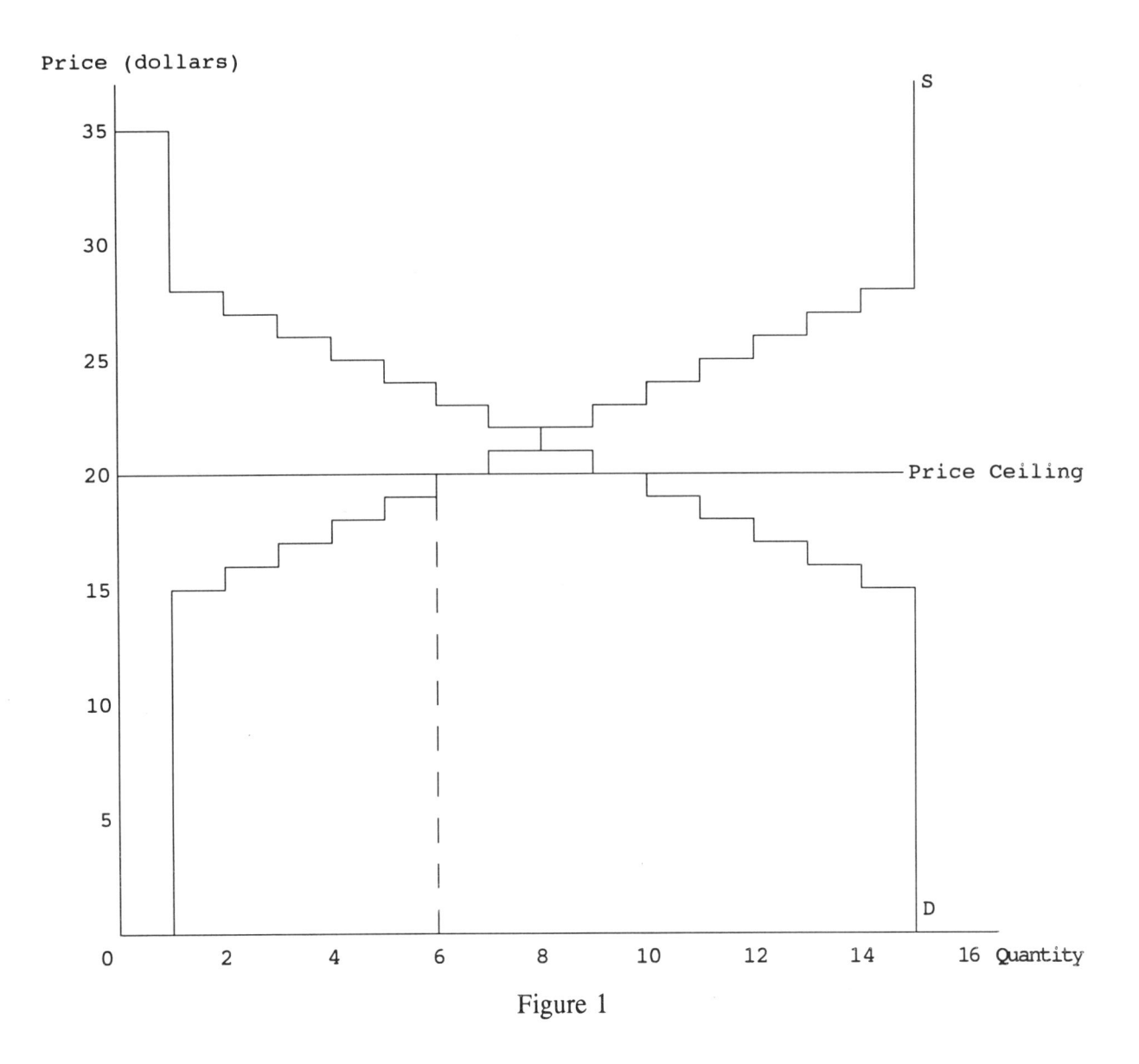

At this point, you are fully equipped with data that can be used to discuss and calculate the deadweight loss from the tax and the incidence of the tax. Compare (or have students compare) the total consumer and producer surplus (that is, the sum of all of their "net benefits") from the last period in which the market was run without the tax with the sum of the consumer and producer surplus *plus* the tax revenue generated during the last period in which the market was run with the tax. The difference is, of course, the deadweight loss of the tax. By comparing the pretax and posttax equilibrium prices, one can observe what share of the tax sellers were able to shift to buyers. This, of course, is the incidence of the tax.

If time permits, impose the same tax on buyers rather than sellers and run the market for several additional periods. If you use our marginal benefit and cost values, the $4 tax on buyers should result in a reduction in the equilibrium quantity from 8 to 6 units (that is, the same effect as an equivalent tax on sellers) and a *decrease* in the equilibrium price from $21-$22 to $19-$20.

Have students compare the total consumer and producer surplus from the last period in which the market was run without the tax with the sum of the consumer and producer surplus *plus* the tax revenue generated during the last period in which the market was run with the tax on buyers. The deadweight loss generated by the tax on buyers should be approximately equal to that generated by the tax on sellers. Similarly, the incidence of the two taxes should be approximately equal.

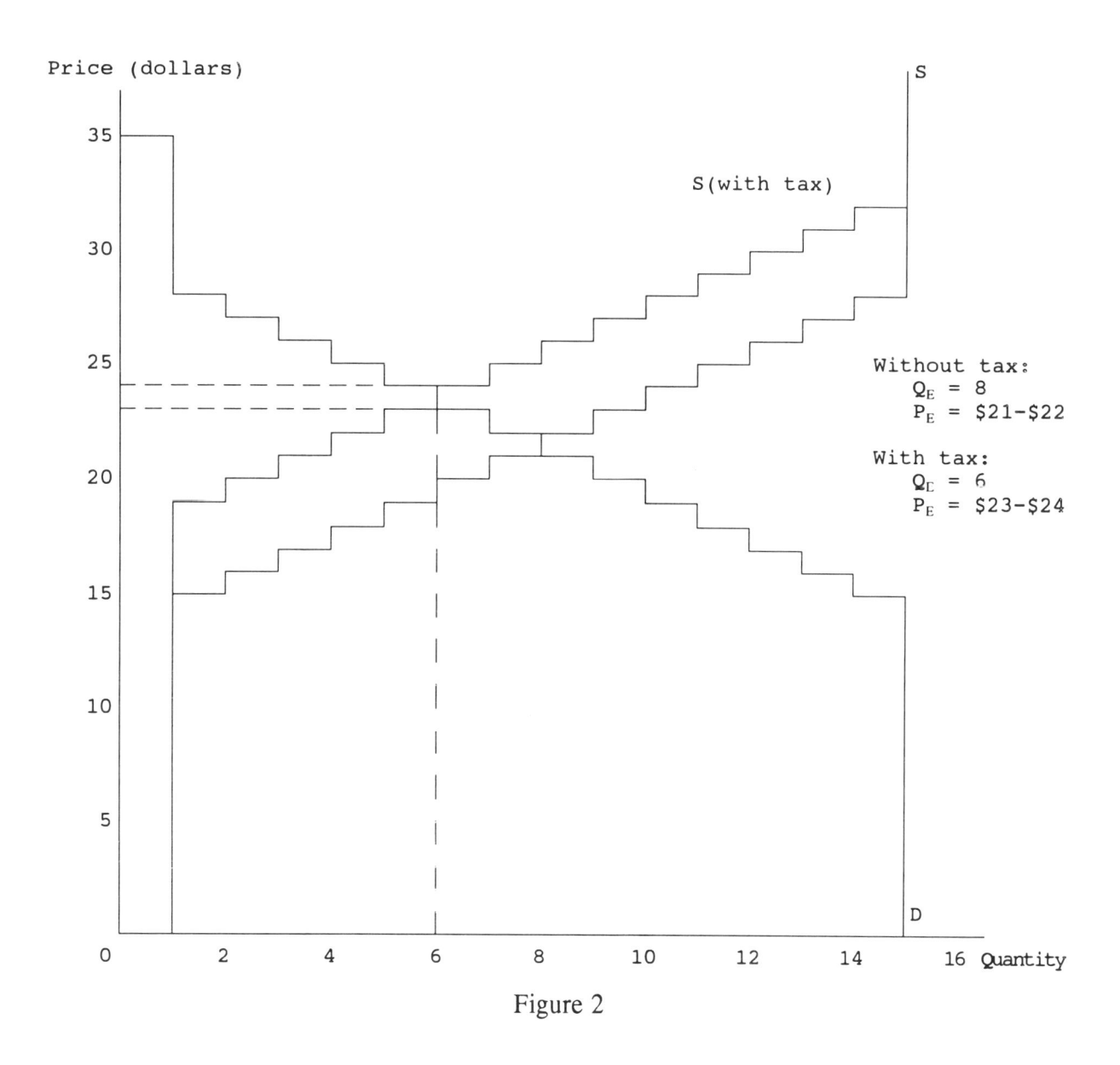

Figure 2

Without tax:
$Q_E = 8$
$P_E = \$21-\$22$

With tax:
$Q_E = 6$
$P_E = \$23-\$24$

Variation 3: Taxes with Perfectly Inelastic Supply or Demand

A final variation of this experiment can be conducted to reinforce the idea that it is the elasticities of supply and demand that determine the incidence of a specific tax, *not* whether the tax is imposed on the buyer or the seller. This variation necessitates the use of different marginal benefit and cost data than in the previous markets. In the first case, suppose that for each of the five sellers the marginal cost of each of the three units that might be produced is $15; for each of the five buyers, the marginal benefit of each of the first two units purchased is $25, while the third unit has no marginal benefit (that is, $0). In the absence of government intervention, the equilibrium quantity and price in this market will be 10 units and $15, respectively (see Figure 3[a]). Now suppose that a specific tax of $5 per unit is imposed on sellers. Although the equilibrium quantity would remain unchanged at 10 units, the equilibrium price would increase by $5 (that is, the full amount of the tax) to $20 (see Figure 3[b]). Sellers could successfully shift the tax, and buyers would bear the entire burden of the tax. If the same tax were imposed on buyers, the equilibrium quantity would remain unchanged at 10 units *and* the equilibrium price would remain unchanged at $15 (see Figure 3[c]). Buyers would again bear the entire burden of the tax. This result occurs, of course, because demand is perfectly inelastic between the old and the new equilibrium points.

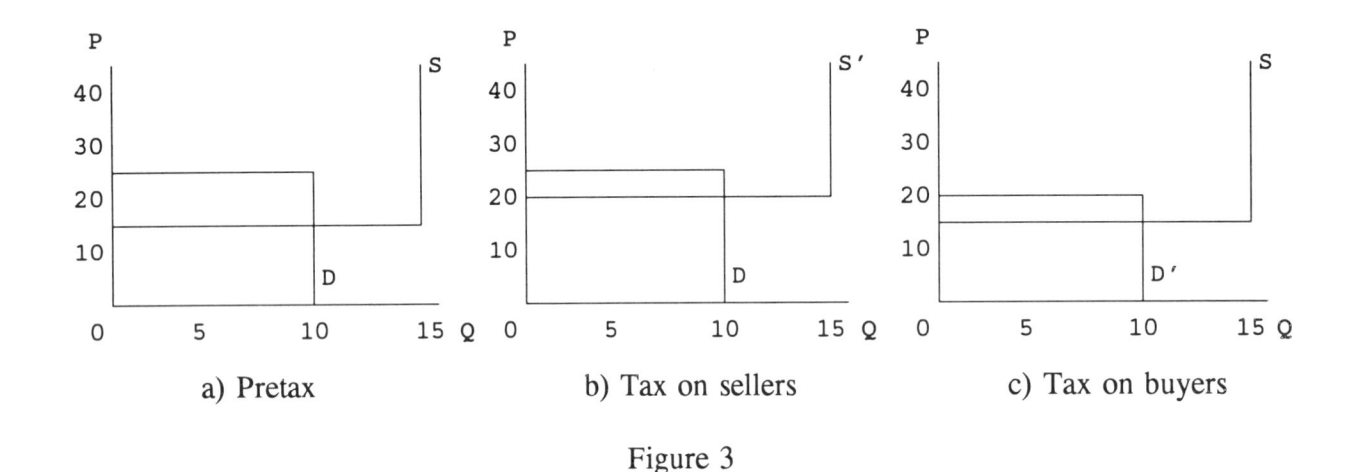

a) Pretax   b) Tax on sellers   c) Tax on buyers

Figure 3

Consider a second case in which each buyer realizes a marginal benefit of $25 for each of the three units that he or she might purchase, while each seller incurs a marginal cost of $15 for each of the first two units produced and sold and a marginal cost of $35 for the third unit produced and sold. In equilibrium, 10 units will be traded at a price of $25 (see Figure 4[a]). If a specific tax of $5 were to be imposed on sellers, the equilibrium quantity and price would be unchanged. The sellers will be unable to shift any portion of the tax to the buyers (see Figure 4[b]). If the tax were instead imposed on the buyers, the equilibrium quantity would remain unchanged, but the equilibrium price would decrease from $25 to $20 (see Figure 4[c]). The buyers would shift the entire $5 tax to the sellers. In either case, sellers would bear the entire burden of the tax. This result occurs whenever supply is perfectly inelastic between the old and the new equilibrium points.

DISCUSSION

The variations described in this experiment demonstrate the versatility of the double oral auction experiment. Although we doubt that any instructor would want to sacrifice the amount

Double Oral Auction with Price Controls/Taxes

of classroom time necessary to conduct all of the variations of the double oral auction just described, the selective use of these variations can be an effective means of reinforcing particular concepts that you might wish to emphasize in your course. It should be possible to conduct the basic double oral auction and one of the variations described above in a single fifty-minute class period.[5] Or if the basic auction was completed previously, it should be possible to complete variation 1 and a significant portion of variation 2 in a single fifty-minute class period.

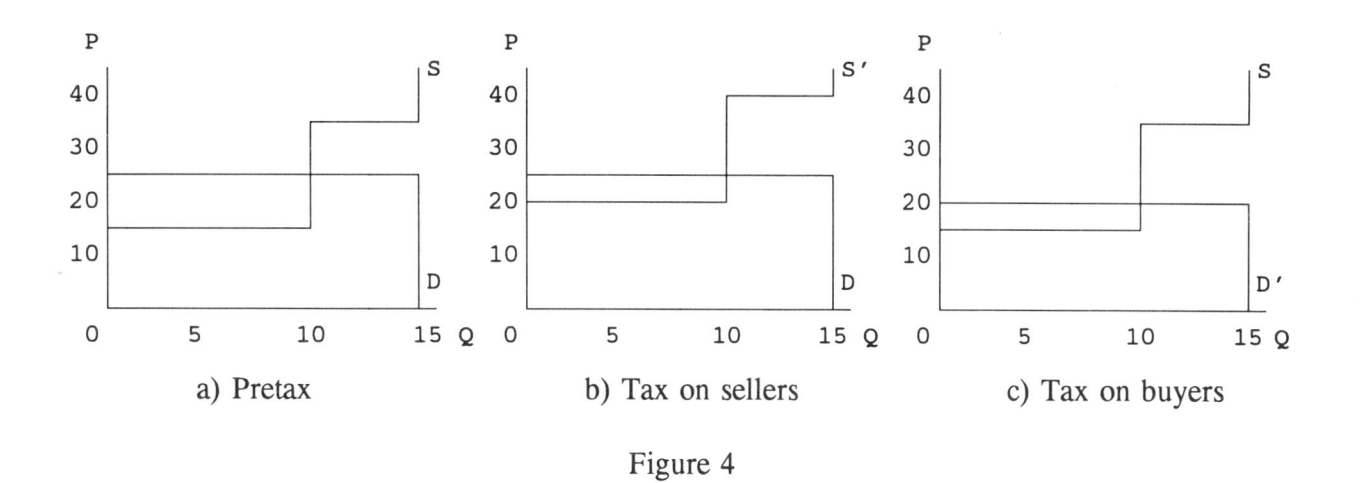

a) Pretax   b) Tax on sellers   c) Tax on buyers

Figure 4

QUESTIONS

To be asked prior to running variation 1 of the experiment:

1. Would the imposition of a price ceiling or the imposition of a price floor be more likely to result in a reduction in the number of units of a product that are traded?

   [Let students speculate on the answer to this question, but let the experiment itself give them the answer. Often students believe that an effective price ceiling will *increase* the number of units sold. They seem to focus on the fact that consumers will want to buy more units of a product if the price is lower; they often overlook the fact that fewer units will be available for sale if a price ceiling is imposed. The correct response is, of course, that the imposition of *either* a price floor or a price ceiling results in a reduction in the number of units traded in a market (provided that the price control were effective, of course, and barring extreme elasticity conditions). Which would result in a larger reduction would depend on the relative slopes of the demand and supply curves.]

---

[5] In the case of variation 2, it should be possible to complete the basic auction and the implementation of a tax on either buyers or sellers. To complete the entire array of treatments described in variation 2 (including those involving extreme elasticity conditions) would almost certainly require several class periods. Of course, the amount of time needed to conduct this experiment will depend largely on how quickly each market converges to the equilibrium. Since convergence usually occurs within three or four periods, the basic auction market and one of the variations can be expected to be completed in the eight periods provided for on the record sheets that follow.

To be asked prior to running variations 2 and/or 3:

2. Suppose that a tax is imposed on the sellers of a good. Will the sellers be able to pass the tax on to the buyers of the product in the form of higher prices?

3. Suppose that a tax is imposed on the buyers of a good. Will the buyers be able to shift the tax to the sellers of the product by demanding lower prices?

[Again, let students speculate on these answers, but let the demonstration markets reveal the answers. Students often believe that sellers can shift taxes, but buyers cannot. The answer, of course, depends on the relative elasticities of supply and demand. Under most conditions, the tax will be partially shifted whether it is imposed on sellers or buyers. Under extreme elasticity conditions, the entire tax may be shifted. After the experiment, it may be worth pointing out that students' intuition about sellers being able to shift taxes may have an empirical basis since excise taxes are most often imposed on products for which the demand is pretty inelastic (for example, gasoline, cigarettes, and alcohol). Hence, in most of the real-world cases that students have had the opportunity to observe, most of the tax probably *was* shifted by sellers (or *not* shifted by buyers).]

REFERENCES/FURTHER READING

Smith, Vernon L. "An Experimental Study of Competitive Market Behavior." Journal of Political Economy (April 1962): 111-137.

_____. "Markets as Economizers of Information: Experimental Examination of the 'Hayek Hypothesis.'" Economic Inquiry (April 1982): 165-179.

APPENDICES TO EXPERIMENT 5

- Instructions for the double oral auction experiment
- Buyers' and sellers' record sheets

Double Oral Auction with Price Controls/Taxes

INSTRUCTIONS

You are about to participate in a market exercise known as a double oral auction. You (and each of the other students who is participating) have been assigned to the role of either buyer or seller. If you are a seller, you have been given a "seller ID" number, which appears on the seller's record sheet that accompanies these instructions. If you are buyer, you have been assigned a "buyer ID" number on the buyer's record sheet that accompanies these instructions. With the exception of your buyer or seller ID number, the information on these sheets is purely private, and you are not to share it with anyone.

This market will operate over a number of "trading periods." If you are a seller, you may make available for sale up to three units during each trading period. Each time that you sell a unit, you incur the marginal cost that is associated with that unit on your seller's record sheet. If you are a buyer, you may buy up to three units during each trading period. Each time you buy a unit, you realize the marginal benefit that is associated with that unit on your buyer's record sheet. Your goal is to maximize your net benefit from selling or buying these units. You need not trade any unit unless you realize a net benefit.

When a trading period opens, sellers and buyers announce the prices at which they are willing to trade a single unit by calling out asks or bids in the following form:

Asks (sellers): "Seller number *n* asks $*xx* for one unit."
Bids (buyers): "Buyer number *n* bids $*xx* for one unit."

Bids and asks are recorded on the blackboard (in sight of all market participants) by the market manager. Once a bid or ask is announced, any new bid must be higher than the previous bid and any new ask must be lower than the previous ask. A unit is traded when a buyer accepts an existing ask (by calling out "Buyer number *n* accepts") or when a seller accepts an existing bid (by calling out "Seller number *n* accepts"). At this point, the buyer and seller involved in the transaction should record the selling/purchase price on their marginal cost/benefit forms and calculate their net benefit from the transaction. The transaction will also be recorded by the market manager for future reference. Once a buyer or seller has sold a particular unit in a trading period, that unit is no longer available for trading, and that buyer or seller should refer to the marginal cost/benefit of their next unit in making subsequent asks or bids during the remainder of the trading period.

After the transaction is recorded, the trading period will continue. The bid/ask/acceptance process will begin again. When bids, asks, and acceptances cease, the market will be closed for the period.

During subsequent trading periods, trading will proceed in the same manner. At the beginning of each trading period, each buyer and seller again has three units to trade, regardless of the number of units he or she was able to trade during the previous period. The number of trading periods will be determined by the market manager.

Remember that as an individual buyer or seller, your goal is to realize the largest possible net benefit over the course of the exercise. This can be accomplished by maximizing the net benefit on each unit that you buy or sell.

BUYERS' RECORD SHEETS

BUYER #1   NAME _____

UNIT BOUGHT	TRADING PERIOD:	1	2	3	4	5	6	7	8
	MARGINAL BENEFIT	$28	$28	$28	$28	$28	$28	$28	$28
1	PURCHASE PRICE	___	___	___	___	___	___	___	___
	NET BENEFIT	___	___	___	___	___	___	___	___
	MARGINAL BENEFIT	$22	$22	$22	$22	$22	$22	$22	$22
2	PURCHASE PRICE	___	___	___	___	___	___	___	___
	NET BENEFIT	___	___	___	___	___	___	___	___
	MARGINAL BENEFIT	$17	$17	$17	$17	$17	$17	$17	$17
3	PURCHASE PRICE	___	___	___	___	___	___	___	___
	NET BENEFIT	___	___	___	___	___	___	___	___

NET BENEFIT (ALL UNITS) ___ ___ ___ ___ ___ ___ ___ ___

NET BENEFIT (ALL PERIODS) ___

BUYER #2   NAME _____

UNIT BOUGHT	TRADING PERIOD:	1	2	3	4	5	6	7	8
	MARGINAL BENEFIT	$35	$35	$35	$35	$35	$35	$35	$35
1	PURCHASE PRICE	___	___	___	___	___	___	___	___
	NET BENEFIT	___	___	___	___	___	___	___	___
	MARGINAL BENEFIT	$20	$20	$20	$20	$20	$20	$20	$20
2	PURCHASE PRICE	___	___	___	___	___	___	___	___
	NET BENEFIT	___	___	___	___	___	___	___	___
	MARGINAL BENEFIT	$18	$18	$18	$18	$18	$18	$18	$18
3	PURCHASE PRICE	___	___	___	___	___	___	___	___
	NET BENEFIT	___	___	___	___	___	___	___	___

NET BENEFIT (ALL UNITS) ___ ___ ___ ___ ___ ___ ___ ___

NET BENEFIT (ALL PERIODS) ___

Double Oral Auction with Price Controls/Taxes

BUYER #3   NAME _____

UNIT BOUGHT	TRADING PERIOD:	1	2	3	4	5	6	7	8
	MARGINAL BENEFIT	$27	$27	$27	$27	$27	$27	$27	$27
1	PURCHASE PRICE	___	___	___	___	___	___	___	___
	NET BENEFIT	___	___	___	___	___	___	___	___
	MARGINAL BENEFIT	$21	$21	$21	$21	$21	$21	$21	$21
2	PURCHASE PRICE	___	___	___	___	___	___	___	___
	NET BENEFIT	___	___	___	___	___	___	___	___
	MARGINAL BENEFIT	$15	$15	$15	$15	$15	$15	$15	$15
3	PURCHASE PRICE	___	___	___	___	___	___	___	___
	NET BENEFIT	___	___	___	___	___	___	___	___

NET BENEFIT (ALL UNITS)   ___ ___ ___ ___ ___ ___ ___ ___

NET BENEFIT (ALL PERIODS)   ___

BUYER #4   NAME _____

UNIT BOUGHT	TRADING PERIOD:	1	2	3	4	5	6	7	8
	MARGINAL BENEFIT	$25	$25	$25	$25	$25	$25	$25	$25
1	PURCHASE PRICE	___	___	___	___	___	___	___	___
	NET BENEFIT	___	___	___	___	___	___	___	___
	MARGINAL BENEFIT	$24	$24	$24	$24	$24	$24	$24	$24
2	PURCHASE PRICE	___	___	___	___	___	___	___	___
	NET BENEFIT	___	___	___	___	___	___	___	___
	MARGINAL BENEFIT	$19	$19	$19	$19	$19	$19	$19	$19
3	PURCHASE PRICE	___	___	___	___	___	___	___	___
	NET BENEFIT	___	___	___	___	___	___	___	___

NET BENEFIT (ALL UNITS)   ___ ___ ___ ___ ___ ___ ___ ___

NET BENEFIT (ALL PERIODS)   ___

BUYER #5   NAME _____

UNIT BOUGHT	TRADING PERIOD:	1	2	3	4	5	6	7	8
1	MARGINAL BENEFIT	$26	$26	$26	$26	$26	$26	$26	$26
	PURCHASE PRICE	___	___	___	___	___	___	___	___
	NET BENEFIT	___	___	___	___	___	___	___	___
2	MARGINAL BENEFIT	$23	$23	$23	$23	$23	$23	$23	$23
	PURCHASE PRICE	___	___	___	___	___	___	___	___
	NET BENEFIT	___	___	___	___	___	___	___	___
3	MARGINAL BENEFIT	$16	$16	$16	$16	$16	$16	$16	$16
	PURCHASE PRICE	___	___	___	___	___	___	___	___
	NET BENEFIT	___	___	___	___	___	___	___	___

NET BENEFIT (ALL UNITS)   ___ ___ ___ ___ ___ ___ ___ ___

NET BENEFIT (ALL PERIODS)   ___

SELLERS' RECORD SHEETS

SELLER #1   NAME _____

UNIT SOLD	TRADING PERIOD:	1	2	3	4	5	6	7	8
1	SELLING PRICE	___	___	___	___	___	___	___	___
	MARGINAL COST	$18	$18	$18	$18	$18	$18	$18	$18
	NET BENEFIT	___	___	___	___	___	___	___	___
2	SELLING PRICE	___	___	___	___	___	___	___	___
	MARGINAL COST	$22	$22	$22	$22	$22	$22	$22	$22
	NET BENEFIT	___	___	___	___	___	___	___	___
3	SELLING PRICE	___	___	___	___	___	___	___	___
	MARGINAL COST	$24	$24	$24	$24	$24	$24	$24	$24
	NET BENEFIT	___	___	___	___	___	___	___	___

NET BENEFIT (ALL UNITS)   ___ ___ ___ ___ ___ ___ ___ ___

NET BENEFIT (ALL PERIODS)   ___

Double Oral Auction with Price Controls/Taxes

```
SELLER #2                                    NAME _____

UNIT
SOLD    TRADING PERIOD:    1      2      3      4      5      6      7      8
-------------------------------------------------------------------------------
        SELLING PRICE     ___    ___    ___    ___    ___    ___    ___    ___

  1     MARGINAL COST    $16    $16    $16    $16    $16    $16    $16    $16

        NET BENEFIT       ___    ___    ___    ___    ___    ___    ___    ___
-------------------------------------------------------------------------------
        SELLING PRICE     ___    ___    ___    ___    ___    ___    ___    ___

  2     MARGINAL COST    $21    $21    $21    $21    $21    $21    $21    $21

        NET BENEFIT       ___    ___    ___    ___    ___    ___    ___    ___
-------------------------------------------------------------------------------
        SELLING PRICE     ___    ___    ___    ___    ___    ___    ___    ___

  3     MARGINAL COST    $25    $25    $25    $25    $25    $25    $25    $25

        NET BENEFIT       ___    ___    ___    ___    ___    ___    ___    ___
-------------------------------------------------------------------------------

        NET BENEFIT (ALL UNITS)   ___   ___   ___   ___   ___   ___   ___   ___

        NET BENEFIT (ALL PERIODS)                                          ___
```

```
SELLER #3                                    NAME _____

UNIT
SOLD    TRADING PERIOD:    1      2      3      4      5      6      7      8
-------------------------------------------------------------------------------
        SELLING PRICE     ___    ___    ___    ___    ___    ___    ___    ___

  1     MARGINAL COST    $ 0    $ 0    $ 0    $ 0    $ 0    $ 0    $ 0    $ 0

        NET BENEFIT       ___    ___    ___    ___    ___    ___    ___    ___
-------------------------------------------------------------------------------
        SELLING PRICE     ___    ___    ___    ___    ___    ___    ___    ___

  2     MARGINAL COST    $19    $19    $19    $19    $19    $19    $19    $19

        NET BENEFIT       ___    ___    ___    ___    ___    ___    ___    ___
-------------------------------------------------------------------------------
        SELLING PRICE     ___    ___    ___    ___    ___    ___    ___    ___

  3     MARGINAL COST    $26    $26    $26    $26    $26    $26    $26    $26

        NET BENEFIT       ___    ___    ___    ___    ___    ___    ___    ___
-------------------------------------------------------------------------------

        NET BENEFIT (ALL UNITS)   ___   ___   ___   ___   ___   ___   ___   ___

        NET BENEFIT (ALL PERIODS)                                          ___
```

SELLER #4   NAME _____

UNIT SOLD	TRADING PERIOD:	1	2	3	4	5	6	7	8
1	SELLING PRICE	___	___	___	___	___	___	___	___
	MARGINAL COST	$15	$15	$15	$15	$15	$15	$15	$15
	NET BENEFIT	___	___	___	___	___	___	___	___
2	SELLING PRICE	___	___	___	___	___	___	___	___
	MARGINAL COST	$23	$23	$23	$23	$23	$23	$23	$23
	NET BENEFIT	___	___	___	___	___	___	___	___
3	SELLING PRICE	___	___	___	___	___	___	___	___
	MARGINAL COST	$28	$28	$28	$28	$28	$28	$28	$28
	NET BENEFIT	___	___	___	___	___	___	___	___

NET BENEFIT (ALL UNIS)   ___ ___ ___ ___ ___ ___ ___ ___

NET BENEFIT (ALL PERIODS)   ___

SELLER #5   NAME _____

UNIT SOLD	TRADING PERIOD:	1	2	3	4	5	6	7	8
1	SELLING PRICE	___	___	___	___	___	___	___	___
	MARGINAL COST	$17	$17	$17	$17	$17	$17	$17	$17
	NET BENEFIT	___	___	___	___	___	___	___	___
2	SELLING PRICE	___	___	___	___	___	___	___	___
	MARGINAL COST	$20	$20	$20	$20	$20	$20	$20	$20
	NET BENEFIT	___	___	___	___	___	___	___	___
3	SELLING PRICE	___	___	___	___	___	___	___	___
	MARGINAL COST	$27	$27	$27	$27	$27	$27	$27	$27
	NET BENEFIT	___	___	___	___	___	___	___	___

NET BENEFIT (ALL UNITS)   ___ ___ ___ ___ ___ ___ ___ ___

NET BENEFIT (ALL PERIODS)   ___

EXPERIMENT 6: THE POSTED OFFER AUCTION

OVERVIEW

Most students have had limited real-world experience with the type of trading that takes place under a double auction setting. They are likely to be more familiar with a market characterized by posted prices such as in most retail markets, where there is an implied "take-it-or-leave-it" arrangement. The following experiment describes a typical posted offer mechanism.[1]

MATERIALS NEEDED

- A large blackboard or other writing surface for the recording of bids and offers
- Buyers' and sellers' record sheets containing marginal benefit and marginal cost schedules to distribute to the market participants
- Slips of paper with a number ranging from 1 to N written down, where N is the number of buyers

ADMINISTERING THE EXPERIMENT

Students participate in a market as buyers or sellers of an unspecified product. After distributing and reviewing the instructions that appear in the Appendices at the end of this experiment with your students, randomly distribute the buyers' and sellers' record sheets (also in the Appendices). Each buyer's record sheet includes a buyer ID (for example, "Buyer #2") and the marginal benefit that accrues to that buyer when each consecutive unit of the product is purchased during any single trading period. Similarly, each seller's record sheet includes a seller ID and the marginal cost that a particular seller incurs when each consecutive unit of the product is produced and sold during any single trading period. These record sheets also provide space in which buyers and sellers can record the price and net benefit (that is, the marginal benefit minus the purchase price for buyers; the selling price minus the marginal cost for sellers) of each unit bought or sold.

Begin a trading period with an announcement that each seller has two minutes in which to choose a price, which he or she records on a seller record sheet. Each seller chooses only a single price, so all sales that a seller makes will be at the same price. After all sellers have chosen prices, collect the decision sheets and record the prices on the blackboard. Use the sellers' ID numbers to identify their prices on the blackboard.

---

[1] This experiment draws heavily from Davis and Holt (1993), Chapter 4.

After the prices are posted, the buyers are given the opportunity to make whatever purchases they desire. Buyers' purchases are made sequentially. The buying order is determined by a random draw (without replacement) from a box containing each individual buyer's ID number written down on a separate slip of paper. The first buyer selected in this way will be asked to indicate a seller and a desired purchase quantity. The designated seller may then accept any part of the buyer's bid by stating the quantity he or she wishes to sell. If the first seller selected will not sell all the units that the buyer wants to purchase, the buyer is free to choose a second seller, and so on.

When the first buyer has made all desired purchases, another slip of paper is drawn from the box, and the buyer indicated by the second draw makes bids in the same manner. The process continues until all buyers have had a chance to make purchases. This completes the trading round. A new trading period commences by having sellers submit new prices, and repeating the preceding process.

As an example of what may happen, suppose that there are two buyers, B1 and B2, and two sellers, S1 and S2, who choose prices of $8 and $11, respectively. These prices would be posted on the blackboard as follows:

Seller	S1	S2
Price	8	11
Buyer		
Buyer		

Suppose that B2 is the first buyer selected to shop and indicates a desire to purchase two units from seller S1, but seller S1 agrees to sell only a single unit. Then B2 can request a purchase from another seller. If S2 agrees to sell a unit, the blackboard would appear as follows:

Seller	S1	S2
Price	8	11
Buyer	B2	B2
Buyer		

When B2 has finished making all desired purchases, another buyer is selected. Suppose that the next buyer, B1, requests to buy two units from seller S1, who declines. Then B2 can request units from seller S2. If S2 agrees to sell only a single unit, the blackboard will look like this:

Seller	S1	S2
Price	8	11
Buyer	B2	B2
Buyer		B1

Since there are only two buyers in this example, the period ends when B1 finishes shopping, and sellers are then given two minutes in which to choose prices for the next period.

DISCUSSION

The demand and supply curves in Figure 1 below are generated from the buyer and seller values contained in the record sheets that appear in the Appendices at the end of this experiment. The equilibrium quantity is 5 units and the equilibrium price is $13-$14.[2]

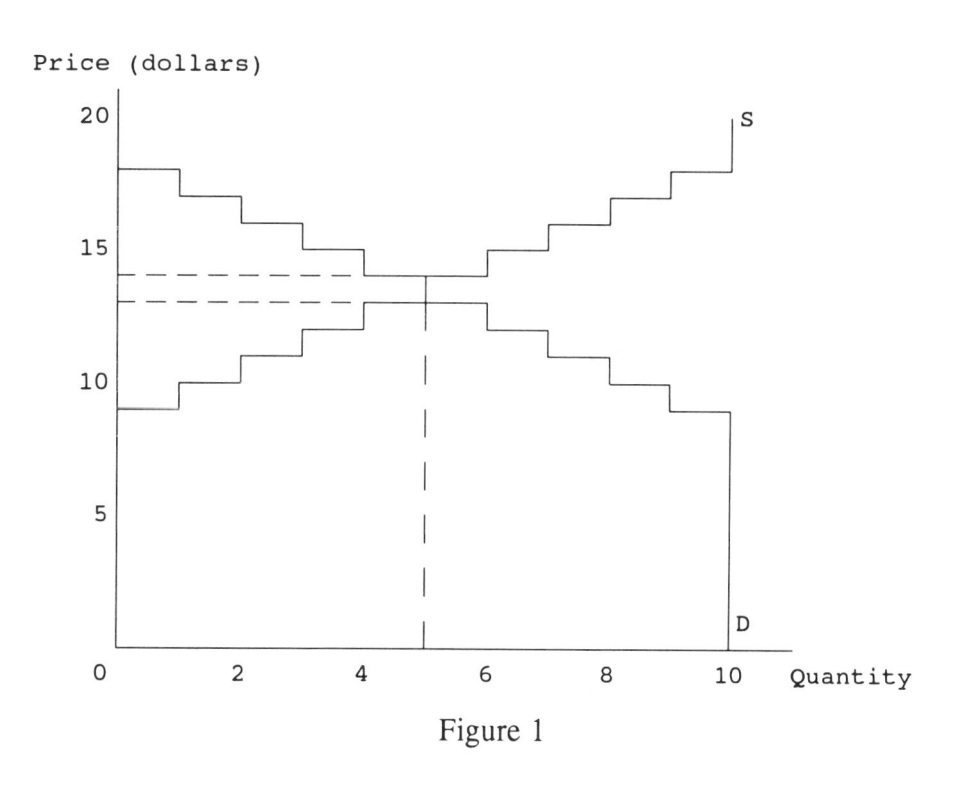

Figure 1

Most instructors are likely to conduct a double oral auction (DOA) prior to the posted-offer auction. This sets up an interesting comparison between the two trading mechanisms in terms of their price and efficiency outcomes, particularly with respect to their convergence properties. The results of the posted-offer auction are typically presented in one of two ways. First, the actual quantity and average price in each period can be compared with the predicted equilibrium price and quantity. Alternatively, the contract prices can be plotted sequentially against the predicted equilibrium price. The latter method is particularly useful in illustrating the difference in convergence properties between the posted-offer and the double oral auctions.

In general, you can expect prices to converge from above the competitive equilibrium price under the posted offer mechanism and to do so a bit more slowly than under the DOA.

---

[2]The $1 range is due to the overlapping steps of the supply and demand curves.

As with the double oral auction, you may introduce a variety of treatments such as price controls and taxes (see Experiment 5 for details). Additional extensions could allow for communication among the sellers so as to allow for explicit collusive behavior or the creation of an outright monopoly situation by designating a single seller with multiple units. Still another variation is to organize a posted-bid auction on behalf of buyers.

QUESTIONS

1. Speculate as to why prices tend to converge to equilibrium from above. Why does convergence take longer than under a double oral auction?

   [The answer is likely to lie in the fact that there is much less information flow between buyer and seller in the posted-offer auction than in the double oral auction.]

2. List several real-world markets that are characterized by the posted-offer mechanism. Why is the posted-offer mechanism used in these markets?

   [Consumer retail markets such as grocery stores, department stores, and fast-food restaurants typically use the posted-price mechanism. The primary reason may be that this mechanism tends to reduce negotiation costs compared to the double oral auction.]

REFERENCES/FURTHER READING

Davis, Douglas D., and Charles Holt. <u>Experimental Economics</u>. Princeton University Press, 1993.

APPENDICES TO EXPERIMENT 6

- Instructions for participants in the posted offer market experiment
- Buyers' record sheets to be distributed to those students who are assigned to the role of buyers
- Sellers' record sheets to be distributed to those students who have been assigned to the role of sellers

STUDENT INSTRUCTIONS

You are about to participate in a market in which some of you will be buyers and others will be sellers. The commodity to be traded is divided into distinct units. We will not specify a name for the commodity; we will simply refer to units.

The market will operate over a number of "trading periods." If you are a seller, you may make available for sale up to two units during each trading period. Each time that you sell a unit, you incur the marginal cost that is associated with that unit on your seller's record sheet. If you are a buyer, you may buy up to two units during each trading period. Each time you buy a unit, you realize the marginal benefit that is associated with that unit on your buyer's record sheet. Your goal is to maximize your net benefit from selling or buying these units. You need not trade any unit unless you realize a net benefit. THE INFORMATION ON YOUR RECORD SHEETS IS PRIVATE. PLEASE DO NOT REVEAL IT TO ANYONE.

Trading Rules

All buyers and sellers have identification numbers; your number is given in the upper part of your record sheet. I will begin each trading period with an announcement that each seller has two minutes in which to choose a price, which he or she will write on a seller record sheet, just below the period number in the column for the current period. Each seller chooses only a single price, so all sales that a seller makes in a given period will be at the same price. After all sellers have chosen prices, the record sheets will be collected and the prices will be written on the blackboard. Sellers' identification numbers will be used to label their prices on the blackboard.

After prices are posted, buyers will be given the opportunity to make whatever purchases they desire. Buyers' bids will be made as follows. I have a box containing each individual buyer's ID number written down on a separate slip of paper. I will hold the box above my head and draw a slip of paper in sequence (without replacement). The first buyer selected in this way will be asked to indicate a seller and a desired purchase quantity. The designated seller will then accept any part of the buyer's bid by stating the quantity he or she wishes to sell. If the first seller selected will not sell all the units that the buyer wants to purchase, the buyer is free to choose a second seller, and so on.

When the first buyer has made all desired purchases, another slip of paper will be drawn from the box, and the buyer indicated by the second draw will make bids in the same manner. The process continues until all buyers have had a chance to make purchases. This completes the trading round. We will reopen the market for a new trading period by having sellers submit new prices, and the process will be repeated.

BUYERS' RECORD SHEETS

===

BUYER #1   NAME _____

UNIT BOUGHT	TRADING PERIOD:	1	2	3	4
	MARGINAL BENEFIT	$18	$18	$18	$18
1	PURCHASE PRICE	____	____	____	____
	NET BENEFIT	____	____	____	____
	MARGINAL BENEFIT	$13	$13	$13	$13
2	PURCHASE PRICE	____	____	____	____
	NET BENEFIT	____	____	____	____
	NET BENEFIT (ALL UNITS)	____	____	____	____
	NET BENEFIT (ALL PERIODS)				____

===

===

BUYER #2   NAME _____

UNIT BOUGHT	TRADING PERIOD:	1	2	3	4
	MARGINAL BENEFIT	$17	$17	$17	$17
1	PURCHASE PRICE	____	____	____	____
	NET BENEFIT	____	____	____	____
	MARGINAL BENEFIT	$12	$12	$12	$12
2	PURCHASE PRICE	____	____	____	____
	NET BENEFIT	____	____	____	____
	NET BENEFIT (ALL UNITS)	____	____	____	____
	NET BENEFIT (ALL PERIODS)				____

===

Posted Offer Auction

```
===============================================================
BUYER #3                                NAME _____

UNIT
BOUGHT   TRADING PERIOD:      1         2         3         4
---------------------------------------------------------------
         MARGINAL BENEFIT    $16       $16       $16       $16

  1      PURCHASE PRICE     _____     _____     _____     _____

         NET BENEFIT        _____     _____     _____     _____
---------------------------------------------------------------
         MARGINAL BENEFIT    $11       $11       $11       $11

  2      PURCHASE PRICE     _____     _____     _____     _____

         NET BENEFIT        _____     _____     _____     _____
---------------------------------------------------------------
      NET BENEFIT (ALL UNITS)   _____  _____    _____     _____

      NET BENEFIT (ALL PERIODS)                           _____
===============================================================


===============================================================
BUYER #4                                NAME _____

UNIT
BOUGHT   TRADING PERIOD:      1         2         3         4
---------------------------------------------------------------
         MARGINAL BENEFIT    $15       $15       $15       $15

  1      PURCHASE PRICE     _____     _____     _____     _____

         NET BENEFIT        _____     _____     _____     _____
---------------------------------------------------------------
         MARGINAL BENEFIT    $10       $10       $10       $10

  2      PURCHASE PRICE     _____     _____     _____     _____

         NET BENEFIT        _____     _____     _____     _____
---------------------------------------------------------------
      NET BENEFIT (ALL UNITS)   _____  _____    _____     _____

      NET BENEFIT (ALL PERIODS)                           _____
===============================================================
```

```
===========================================================================
BUYER #5                                       NAME _____

UNIT
BOUGHT    TRADING PERIOD:      1         2         3         4
---------------------------------------------------------------------------
          MARGINAL BENEFIT    $14       $14       $14       $14

  1       PURCHASE PRICE     _____     _____     _____     _____

          NET BENEFIT        _____     _____     _____     _____
---------------------------------------------------------------------------
          MARGINAL BENEFIT    $ 9       $ 9       $ 9       $ 9

  2       PURCHASE PRICE     _____     _____     _____     _____

          NET BENEFIT        _____     _____     _____     _____
---------------------------------------------------------------------------
          NET BENEFIT (ALL UNITS)   _____   _____   _____   _____

          NET BENEFIT (ALL PERIODS)                         _____
===========================================================================
```

SELLERS' RECORD SHEETS

```
===========================================================================
SELLER #1                                      NAME _____

UNIT
SOLD      TRADING PERIOD:      1         2         3         4
---------------------------------------------------------------------------
          SELLING PRICE      _____     _____     _____     _____

  1       MARGINAL COST       $ 9       $ 9       $ 9       $ 9

          NET BENEFIT        _____     _____     _____     _____
---------------------------------------------------------------------------
          SELLING PRICE      _____     _____     _____     _____

  2       MARGINAL COST      $14       $14       $14       $14

          NET BENEFIT        _____     _____     _____     _____
---------------------------------------------------------------------------
          NET BENEFIT (ALL UNITS)   _____   _____   _____   _____

          NET BENEFIT (ALL PERIODS)                         _____
===========================================================================
```

Posted Offer Auction

```
================================================================
SELLER #2                              NAME _____

UNIT
SOLD    TRADING PERIOD:     1         2         3         4
        ---------------------------------------------------------
        SELLING PRICE     ____      ____      ____      ____
  1     MARGINAL COST     $10       $10       $10       $10
        ---------------------------------------------------------
        NET BENEFIT       ____      ____      ____      ____
------------------------------------------------------------------
        SELLING PRICE     ____      ____      ____      ____
  2     MARGINAL COST     $15       $15       $15       $15
        ---------------------------------------------------------
        NET BENEFIT       ____      ____      ____      ____
------------------------------------------------------------------
        NET BENEFIT (ALL UNITS)  ____   ____   ____   ____

        NET BENEFIT (ALL PERIODS)                        ____
==================================================================


==================================================================
SELLER #3                              NAME _____

UNIT
SOLD    TRADING PERIOD:     1         2         3         4
        ---------------------------------------------------------
        SELLING PRICE     ____      ____      ____      ____
  1     MARGINAL COST     $11       $11       $11       $11
        ---------------------------------------------------------
        NET BENEFIT       ____      ____      ____      ____
------------------------------------------------------------------
        SELLING PRICE     ____      ____      ____      ____
  2     MARGINAL COST     $16       $16       $16       $16
        ---------------------------------------------------------
        NET BENEFIT       ____      ____      ____      ____
------------------------------------------------------------------
        NET BENEFIT (ALL UNITS)  ____   ____   ____   ____

        NET BENEFIT (ALL PERIODS)                        ____
==================================================================
```

```
===============================================================
SELLER #4                              NAME _____

UNIT
SOLD      TRADING PERIOD:     1        2         3         4
          ---------------------------------------------------
          SELLING PRICE      ____     ____      ____      ____

  1       MARGINAL COST      $12      $12       $12       $12
          ---------------------------------------------------
          NET BENEFIT        ____     ____      ____      ____
---------------------------------------------------------------
          SELLING PRICE      ____     ____      ____      ____

  2       MARGINAL COST      $17      $17       $17       $17
          ---------------------------------------------------
          NET BENEFIT        ____     ____      ____      ____
---------------------------------------------------------------
      NET BENEFIT (ALL UNITS)  ____    ____      ____      ____

      NET BENEFIT (ALL PERIODS)                                ____
===============================================================


===============================================================
SELLER #5                              NAME _____

UNIT
SOLD      TRADING PERIOD:     1        2         3         4
          ---------------------------------------------------
          SELLING PRICE      ____     ____      ____      ____

  1       MARGINAL COST      $13      $13       $13       $13
          ---------------------------------------------------
          NET BENEFIT        ____     ____      ____      ____
---------------------------------------------------------------
          SELLING PRICE      ____     ____      ____      ____

  2       MARGINAL COST      $18      $18       $18       $18
          ---------------------------------------------------
          NET BENEFIT        ____     ____      ____      ____
---------------------------------------------------------------
      NET BENEFIT (ALL UNITS)  ____    ____      ____      ____

      NET BENEFIT (ALL PERIODS)                                ____
===============================================================
```

EXPERIMENT 7: WIDGET PRODUCTION AND COST

OVERVIEW

Many students find the standard principles-level treatment of production and cost to be an incomprehensible maze of definitions and formulas, all of which can be very difficult to relate to real-world production relationships. In the following exercise (which is similar in method to Experiment 1), students generate their own short-run production data and apply the relevant production and cost concepts directly to this data.[1] Students who complete this exercise should have a better understanding of the relationship between these production and cost concepts and their real-world counterparts. Although the length of this exercise is somewhat open-ended, the first part of the exercise (in which students produce a commodity) should take no more than fifteen minutes (including the introduction, instructions, and production). The calculation of production and cost data should take no more than another fifteen minutes of class time (provided that the production and cost concepts have been defined beforehand), or it can be assigned as homework.

MATERIALS NEEDED

- A work surface (half of the desk or table at the front of the classroom works fine)
- A stapler and supply of staples
- Paper (8.5" x 11" sheets that have been cut in half prior to class)
- Handouts for use in recording and calculating the production and cost data

ADMINISTERING THE EXPERIMENT

Distribute a copy of the handout (reproduced in the Appendices at the end of this experiment) to each student. Then describe the nature of the inputs that will be used during the experiment. The capital input is comprised of a work surface, paper, and a loaded stapler, while labor will be provided by students. Together, these inputs produce widgets. A widget is produced by folding a sheet of paper twice and stapling it. Student should be warned that widgets are quite fragile and break if they fall onto the floor at any time during the production process.

The production of widgets proceeds over a number of periods of a set length (forty-five seconds is usually adequate). In each period, the fixed capital is combined with an increasing number of units of labor. One unit of labor consists of one student working for one production

---

[1] This experiment is adapted from Neral and Ray (1995).

period (that is, forty-five seconds). We suggest that you run the first production period with *zero* units of labor (but be prepared for some curious looks from your students as you wait to observe how many widgets will be produced with no units of labor in forty-five seconds).[2] At the end of the period, record the number of units of labor employed and the number of widgets produced during the period on the blackboard or on a transparency (see the Appendices that follow for a transparency master) and have students do the same on the handout under the columns headed "L" (labor) and "TPP" (total physical product). At this point, ask for a student to volunteer to provide labor to produce widgets in the next production period. After making certain that the student understands how widgets are produced, start the second production period by saying "Go." Forty-five seconds later, say "Stop." Count the widgets that were produced during the second period, record the relevant input and output data on the blackboard (or the transparency), and have students record the same data on the handouts. Continue the exercise for several more periods, employing one additional unit of labor in each succeeding period.

Ideally, the exercise should be terminated after *diminishing* marginal returns have set in, but before *negative* marginal returns have set in. This usually means running the exercise for four or five periods, but the number of periods will vary with the particular group of students and the size of the work surface provided.[3] If you continue to increase the amount of labor until negative returns set in, you'll have to spend some time explaining why some of our formulas (for example, $\Delta TC/\Delta Q$) don't work very well with negative changes in output.

Once the levels of labor input and their associated total physical products of widgets are observed, the calculation of average and marginal physical products is routine. If the prices per unit of capital and labor are specified ($10 and $5 seem to work pretty well for us), students can proceed with the calculation of total, average, and marginal costs.

DISCUSSION

This exercise provides a quick and effective way of putting some empirical flesh on the theoretical bones of production and cost theory. Although the calculations at the end of the exercise are routine, they cease to be a mere plugging of data into formulas. The concept of marginal physical product should become clearer to most students when they realize that the marginal physical product of the third unit of labor is simply the increase in output that resulted when the third student was brought into the exercise. Likewise, the cost concepts can be related to the production process that has just been observed, making the relationship between the production and cost concepts more clear.

A word of caution is in order at this point. Students who participate in this exercise will exhibit dramatically different levels of motivation, physical coordination, and, hence, marginal

---

[2]To maximize the entertainment value of the exercise, we suggest that you emphatically announce "GO!" at the beginning of the period and "STOP!" forty-five seconds later during this first period (and in each succeeding period, for that matter).

[3]The smaller the work surface, the more quickly congestion and diminishing returns will set in.

Widget Production and Cost   63

productivity. As a result, graphing the production and cost curves generated by this exercise may generate bizarre results. However, it may be possible to reduce this problem somewhat through the use of "creative timekeeping" during the course of the production exercise. This is simply a matter of counting the number of times you hear the stapler used during a particular period and then adjusting the length of the current period upward or downward slightly so that the exercise generates the desired results (say, increasing marginal returns due to specialization in early periods followed by decreasing marginal returns due to congestion in later periods). As long as these "dynamic adjustments" are small (say, five seconds or less), students are unlikely to notice them and you may be able to avoid spending time explaining why the textbook theory did not perfectly describe the data generated in the classroom. And even if you employ this bit of deviousness, you may still occasionally encounter cases where you are unable to make the cost curves generated by the exercise look like the cost curves contained in the textbook. Fortunately, a moment's glance at the cost data will reveal when this is the case and allow you to suggest to your students that they need *not* try to use the data generated during the exercise to graph actual production and cost curves.

QUESTIONS

1. What would have happened to the quantity of widgets produced if additional units of labor had continued to be added? (This question should be asked only if the exercise was terminated *before* the marginal physical product of labor became negative.)

   [As additional labor was added, the marginal productivity of labor would continue to decrease, eventually becoming negative. Because the amount of capital is fixed, congestion would eventually result in a decrease in the quantity of widgets produced.]

2. What is the relationship between the marginal productivity of labor and the marginal cost of production of widgets?

   [There is an inverse relationship between these two variables. As long as the marginal physical product of labor is increasing, the marginal cost of widgets is decreasing. When the marginal physical product of labor decreases, the marginal cost of widgets increases.]

REFERENCES/FURTHER READING

Neral, John, and Margaret Ray. "Experiential Learning in the Undergraduate Classroom: Two Exercises." Economic Inquiry (January 1995): 170-174.

APPENDICES TO EXPERIMENT 7

- Student handout
- Transparency master for recording production and cost data

PRODUCTION AND COST

Inputs: capital: paper, work surface, and stapler (fixed), labor (variable)

To produce: widgets: fold paper twice, staple

Assume: price of capital = $10/unit, price of labor = $5/unit

K	L	Q	AP_L	MP_L	FC	VC	TC	MC	AFC	AVC	ATC
1	___	___	___		___	___	___		___	___	___
1	___	___	___	___	___	___	___	___	___	___	___
1	___	___	___	___	___	___	___	___	___	___	___
1	___	___	___	___	___	___	___	___	___	___	___
1	___	___	___	___	___	___	___	___	___	___	___
1	___	___	___	___	___	___	___	___	___	___	___
1	___	___	___	___	___	___	___	___	___	___	___
1	___	___	___	___	___	___	___	___	___	___	___

PRODUCTION AND COST

Inputs capital: paper, work surface, and stapler (fixed), labor (variable)
To produce: widgets: fold paper twice, staple
Assume price of capital = $10/unit, price of labor = $5/unit

K	L	Q	AP_L	MP_L	FC	VC	TC	MC	AFC	AVC	ATC
1	_	_	_	_	_	_	_	_	_	_	_
1	_	_	_	_	_	_	_	_	_	_	_
1	_	_	_	_	_	_	_	_	_	_	_
1	_	_	_	_	_	_	_	_	_	_	_
1	_	_	_	_	_	_	_	_	_	_	_
1	_	_	_	_	_	_	_	_	_	_	_
1	_	_	_	_	_	_	_	_	_	_	_
1	_	_	_	_	_	_	_	_	_	_	_

EXPERIMENT 8: THE DOLLAR AUCTION

OVERVIEW

The concepts of sunk and marginal costs can be difficult to get across to students. The following experiment involves auctioning dollar bills to students under a strict "all bidders must pay" rule. The auction induces a game of escalation in which bidders attempt to minimize their losses.[1]

MATERIALS NEEDED

- An ample supply of crisp one-dollar bills

ADMINISTERING THE EXPERIMENT

Tell the students that you will be auctioning dollar bills the next class period and to bring change if they are interested in participating. Impress upon them that there is no catch--you will be auctioning off genuine U.S. one-dollar bills, each bill will be sold to the highest bidder, and you will auction off at least two dollar bills--more if there is sufficient interest.

On the day of the auction, show the students the stack of crisp, new one-dollar bills that you will be selling. Choose an assistant from among the nonbidders to keep track of individual bids and then explain the rules of the auction.

The auction is conducted as an English auction, with the highest bidder taking the dollar bill. Each time a player bids, his or her bid is recorded by the assistant. If a player bids more than once, the higher bid replaces the lower bid, so that a player always has only one outstanding bid. As opposed to a standard English auction however, the winning bidder is not the only bidder who pays for the dollar. When the auction ends, all bidders who entered a bid during the auction must pay an amount equal to their highest bid. Only the highest bidder, however, gets the dollar. Once these rules are explained, you may begin auctioning the first dollar.

DISCUSSION

Predictably enough, the auction generally starts with a bid of a penny or two. Bids then slowly approach $.50, $.90, and then $1. The person who bids $.99 only to be outbid at $1,

---

[1] This is an edited version of an experiment that Michael Haupert contributed to the Spring, 1994, issue of *Classroom Expernomics*.

hesitates a few seconds before realizing that bidding $1.01 for a dollar is not such a crazy idea. She realizes that if she stops now, she will have spent $.99 for nothing; whereas spending only $.02 more may net her a dollar. The first bidder to go over a dollar generally elicits a roar of laughter from the class, which appreciates it even more as the bidding escalates further.

After auctioning off the first dollar you may want to ask the bidders what their strategies were and why they would pay more than $1 for a dollar. Invariably, you will find students talking about comparing marginal (versus sunk) costs and marginal benefits (though not using those precise terms).

After a few purchases, the bidders begin to scheme and wonder aloud about the possibility of colluding in order to depress prices. As a variation to the preceding rules you may want to encourage collusion (or at the least not discourage collusion) by, say, leaving the room so they may plot strategy. When you return to the room, it takes only a few bids before the collusion breaks down and price escalates beyond a dollar. This leads to a very interesting discussion about collusion and cartels and the difficulty of maintaining them.

After the auction, you are likely to find yourself in possession of a rather large sum of cash. After reimbursing yourself for your outlay of dollars, inform the class that you will return the rest of the money to them, but they must decide how to divide it up. Do not tell them before the auction begins that you will return any money. Inform them of this only when you have auctioned the last bill. Their decision on how to divide the money usually leads to yet another discussion, this one on allocation. Should only those who participated in the auction receive the money (usually one of the first criteria suggested)? Should the money be divided equally? Should only those who lost money or did not get a dollar receive money? Should a lottery determine who receives the money?

QUESTIONS

1. In what ways can U.S. involvement in the Vietnam War be described as an example of the dollar auction?

   [A common argument heard during the war was that, since the U.S. had already invested so much in terms of dollars and lives, to pull out before the war was won would cause us to have "wasted" all those dollars and lives. This can be interpreted as either a "win-at-all-cost" strategy or some form of regret over sunk costs.]

2. Can you think of other settings where there is a tendency on the part of participants to escalate their activities?

   [The British experience with cost-overruns while building the Concorde jet comes to mind.]

REFERENCES/FURTHER READING

Haupert, Michael J. "Sunk Cost and Marginal Cost." Classroom Expernomics (Spring 1994): 6-7.

EXPERIMENT 9: A PRICE-SEARCHING EXPERIMENT

OVERVIEW

The following experiment places students in the position of price-searching monopolists facing an unknown demand curve.[1] Through an iterative search process, students attempt to discover the nature of the market demand curve and, ultimately, the profit-maximizing price/quantity combination. Although instructors may emphasize the application of marginal analysis in determining the optimal price/quantity combination, students usually utilize a variety of search strategies--all of which are fodder for classroom discussion.

MATERIALS NEEDED

- Student handouts containing record forms and cost information

ADMINISTERING THE EXPERIMENT

Students should participate in the price-searching experiment after being exposed to the basic concepts of demand, supply, and cost, but before any discussion of the formal analytical determination of a price-searching firm's profit-maximizing choice of output and price.[2]

To begin, present the students with a brief set of instructions (see the Appendices at the end of this experiment) describing the nature of their task: to attempt to maximize profit in a market where they are the only seller and have full knowledge of their production costs (see the Appendices) but must learn about the nature of the demand for their product solely through their experiences in the market.

The experiment is divided into two five-period stages: a "free search" stage that does not count toward the student's grade, and the final stage, which is used to evaluate the student's performance relative to other students with the same demand and cost conditions.

During each market period, the student submits his or her record sheet to the instructor with a production quantity and an offer price entered on the appropriate line. The instructor uses an integer-discrete demand function (see the Appendices at the end of this experiment) to

---

[1] This experiment is adapted from Wells (1991).

[2] A computerized version of this experiment, known as MONOP, has been developed by the Economic Science Laboratory at the University of Arizona. For details on procuring a copy, contact Shawn LaMaster, Economic Science Laboratory, University of Arizona, Tucson, AZ 85721.

calculate the actual quantity sold at the offer price and enters the amount on the student's record sheet. The record sheet is returned to the student so that he or she may calculate total revenue and profit in preparation for the next period. The process repeats until the experiment is completed.

As an example, consider Figure 1 which contains the demand, marginal revenue, and marginal cost curves based upon the information contained in the appendices. The profit-maximizing price is $20.50 and the profit-maximizing quantity is 12 units. At this price quantity combination, a student could earn a profit of $174 per period. Suppose that a student submitted a price of $24.25 and a quantity of 10 units. From the demand schedule in the appendices, you can see that the student will be able to sell only 4 units. The fourth unit will be sold because the price is below $24.50; the fifth unit would be sold only if the price were $24 or less. Hence, the student will generate a total revenue of $97 and will incur a total cost of $49 for a profit of $48.

DISCUSSION

After participating in the experiment, students are likely to be more receptive to learning the analytical approach to solving for the profit-maximizing monopoly price and output. Indeed, your students may be eager to apply their newly learned skills in an additional experiment (run with different underlying demand and/or cost structures).

Do not be surprised at the lack of sophistication in terms of the search strategies employed by your students. As Wells (1991) describes, even students with a strong classroom experience with marginal analysis will find it difficult to reason in marginal terms. Few students will devise a search strategy based on equating marginal revenue with marginal cost. Most students seem to think in terms of "totals" and "averages."

When demand is not revealed, the few students who attempt to establish a marginal revenue schedule experience several difficulties. First, students will generally encounter some confusion over the shape of the demand curve due to its discreteness when, for example, over some price ranges, a price increase (or decrease) leads to no change in quantity demanded. Second, if price is decreased and total revenue increases, students perceive marginal revenue as positive, but, over the same range, if price is increased and total revenue falls, they conclude that marginal revenue is negative. The confusion is primarily due to the definition of marginal revenue as the change in revenue from selling an additional unit of output. In the experiment, students naturally both raise and lower price as they search for the profit-maximizing level of output. These problems might appear to be trivial, but to students they are a major impediment in establishing marginal revenue.

Indeed, given the difficulty with using the marginal approach to solving for the profit-maximizing output, you may find students reluctant to make price changes during the final five market periods (when they are being judged on their profitability). If they have discovered a price/quantity combination that they think yields a satisfactory level of profits, they may tend

A Price-Searching Experiment

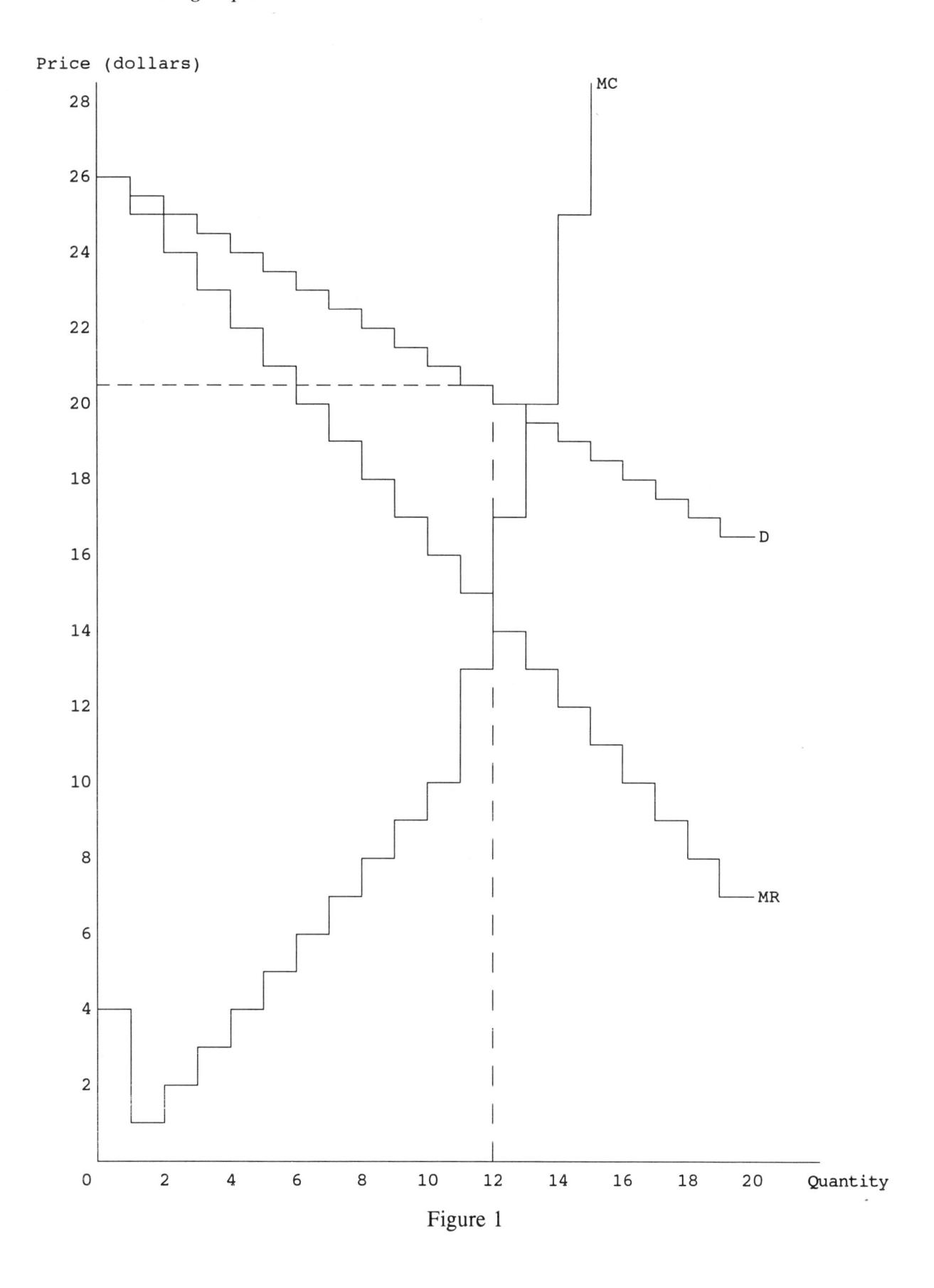

Price (dollars)

Figure 1

to repeat that combination throughout the remaining market periods. As Wells (1991) has observed, "Uncertainty and fear of losing profits seem to be a rationale for price rigidity."

Finally, like the double oral auction, this experiment offers opportunities for numerous permutations. Cost conditions can easily be changed, or demand shifts may be introduced. Students could also be offered the opportunity to purchase information about demand. For example, students might incur a cost for each round of the trial stage that they use to obtain information about the market.

QUESTIONS

1. Plot the marginal and average cost curves implied from your total cost schedule.

2. To the best of your ability, sketch the demand curve as revealed to you during your price search. Sketch the marginal revenue curve.

3. What is the profit-maximizing output and price based on your sketches?

    [Compare student answers to the $20.50 and 12 units generated by the given demand and cost information.]

4. How would you change your price/quantity offer if your fixed cost increased by $10? If your total cost increased by $10 per unit?

    [An increase in fixed costs should not alter the profit-maximizing price-quantity combination since the underlying marginal conditions are unaltered. However, an increase in per unit costs will increase the marginal costs of production which, in turn, will reduce the optimal output and raise the price.]

REFERENCES/FURTHER READING

Wells, Donald A. "Laboratory Experiments for Undergraduate Instruction in Economics." Journal of Economic Education (Summer 1991): 293-300.

APPENDICES TO EXPERIMENT 9

- Demand and cost information
- Student instructions
- Student cost information
- Student worksheet

A Price-Searching Experiment

DEMAND AND COST INFORMATION

Unit	Demand Price	Marginal Revenue	Marginal Cost
1	$26.00	26.00	4.00
2	25.50	25.00	1.00
3	25.00	24.00	2.00
4	24.50	23.00	3.00
5	24.00	22.00	4.00
6	23.50	21.00	5.00
7	23.00	20.00	6.00
8	22.50	19.00	7.00
9	22.00	18.00	8.00
10	21.50	17.00	9.00
11	21.00	16.00	10.00
12	20.50	15.00	13.00
13	20.00	14.00	17.00
14	19.50	13.00	20.00
15	19.00	12.00	25.00
16	18.50	11.00	30.00
17	18.00	10.00	40.00
18	17.50	9.00	50.00
19	17.00	8.00	60.00
20	16.50	7.00	70.00

The instructor uses this information to determine the number of units that will be demanded at the price selected by the student in each period. This table is *not* to be provided to students.

STUDENT INSTRUCTIONS

Members of the class will participate in an economics experiment to earn extra credit. Each of you will be placed in a market situation as a monopolist where you attempt to earn the highest possible level of profits.

The amount of extra credit you earn will depend on how well you do in the experiment. You will be judged on the basis of a) how much profit you earn relative to other members of the class in the same market and b) on your approach to decision-making. For the latter, systematic price searching will be rewarded rather than luck. When you participate in the experiment, keep a written record of your calculations of demand, marginal revenue, and the profit-maximizing price and quantity. The results of your calculations also should be shown on graph paper. Include the calculations as part of your notebook.

As a seller, you are familiar with your costs. However, you are not provided with information about consumer demand, but rather must search for this information. For this purpose, you will utilize five trial market periods to determine how consumers respond to prices and the quantities you offer. These trial periods do not count in the calculation of the profits you have earned. You will be judged by your performance on the final five rounds.

For each round, you will choose a price and the quantity you offer for sale. Your instructor will inform you of the number of units you sold at that price. You will use this information to determine demand conditions during the trial market periods and to calculate the profit you have earned during the final five market periods.

A Price-Searching Experiment

STUDENT COST INFORMATION

Units Offered	Total Cost
0	25
1	29
2	30
3	32
4	35
5	39
6	44
7	50
8	57
9	65
10	74
11	84
12	97
13	114
14	134
15	161
16	191
17	231
18	281
19	341
20	411

STUDENT WORKSHEET

Trial Market Periods

Period	Price	Quantity Offered	Quantity Sold	Total Revenue	Total Costs	Profit
1						
2						
3						
4						
5						

Final Market Periods

Period	Price	Quantity Offered	Quantity Sold	Total Revenue	Total Costs	Profit
6						
7						
8						
9						
10						

Note: This is your private information. Do not reveal this information to anyone else. Your bonus-point ranking may suffer if you do.

EXPERIMENT 10: OLIGOPOLY, INTERDEPENDENCE, AND COLLUSION (I)

OVERVIEW

There are a number of classroom experiments designed to illustrate the difficulties inherent in any effort to formulate and maintain collusive agreements in imperfectly competitive markets. As Taylor points out in Chapter 11 of *Economics*, there may be a strong incentive to defect from such agreements, since those parties who cheat on the agreements achieve higher profits than those who adhere to the agreements. The following experiment[1] utilizes an *n*-person prisoner's dilemma to put students in a situation similar to that of cartel members (for example, OPEC members who have entered into an agreement to adhere to production quotas in order to raise the market price of their product). Although adherence to the agreement increases the profits of all members, any individual member who defects from the agreement achieves an even higher profit. As the number of defectors increases, however, the total profits of the cartel decrease.

Students in this game make their decisions privately. Like real-world cartel members, defectors may eventually be found out, but they need not publicly announce that they are cheating on the cartel agreement. Hence, while it may be clear that *someone* is cheating on the agreement, the identity of the defectors is not public knowledge.

MATERIALS NEEDED

- Instructions, record sheets, and decision sheets for distribution to the class

ADMINISTERING THE EXPERIMENT

In this experiment, students play a game (see Table 1) for a number of periods to be determined by the instructor. Begin by putting the table showing the payoffs for the game on the blackboard (or use the transparency master provided in the Appendices that follow). Distribute the instructions, record sheets, and decision sheets[2] to the class (all found in the Appendices). Read the instructions aloud, answering any questions about the rules of the game,

---

[1] This experiment grew out of experimental research conducted by Mark Isaac, Charles Plott, and James Walker to examine voluntary contribution mechanisms in the provision of public goods. This particular version of the game is the work of Raymond Batallio of Texas A&M University.

[2] We suggest stapling a number of decision sheets (equal to the maximum number of rounds that you intend to complete) directly onto the front of each student's record sheet. The Decision Sheets page in the Appendices section contains four decision sheets. It should be duplicated and the individual forms separated and attached to the record sheet prior to running the experiment.

but do not discuss the relative advantages or disadvantages of any particular strategy.[3] Emphasize the fact that communication between students during the experiment is strictly prohibited. A brief description of the game follows.

In each round of the game, each student must select either "0" or "1." The payoff for each student depends upon whether that student has selected "0" or "1" *and* the total number of students who have selected "1." For example, if ten students select "1" and the remaining students select "0" in a particular round, those students who have selected "1" receive a payoff of $.40 and those students who have selected "0" receive a payoff of $.90 for the round. If twenty students select "1" in a round, then those students who have selected "1" receive a payoff of $.80 and those students who have selected "0" receive a payoff of $1.30.

In the early rounds of the experiment, a significant but decreasing number of students will usually select "1." But as these students come to realize that individuals who select "0" always receive $.50 more than those who select "1," the number of students selecting "1" will decrease rapidly. As a result, the actual payoffs being earned by the students will be much smaller than would be possible if everyone selected "1."

At this point your students, convinced that their inability to communicate with each other is a major barrier to achieving higher payoffs, will respond enthusiastically if you repeal the rule that restricts communication between students. Some student will quickly point out to the others that everyone could earn a much higher payoff if everyone selected "1."

Number of People Choosing "1"	Payoff for Those Choosing "1"	"0"
0	$ .00	$ .50
1	.04	.54
2	.08	.58
3	.12	.62
4	.16	.66
5	.20	.70
6	.24	.74
7	.28	.78
8	.32	.82
9	.36	.86
10	.40	.90
11	.44	.94
12	.48	.98
13	.52	1.02
14	.56	1.06
15	.60	1.10
16	.64	1.14
17	.68	1.18
18	.72	1.22
19	.76	1.26
20	.80	1.30
21	.84	1.34
22	.88	1.38
23	.92	1.42
24	.96	1.46
25	1.00	1.50
26	1.04	1.54
27	1.08	1.58
28	1.12	1.62
29	1.16	1.66
30	1.20	1.70

Table 1

---

[3]It might also be wise to inform students that they are not playing for real money, but for the satisfaction of accumulating the highest possible payoff (or for bonus points, if you prefer).

A spirited discussion is likely to ensue, usually culminating in an agreement that everyone will select "1" in the next round. But since the agreement doesn't alter the underlying strategic nature of the game, the cartel agreement will be only partially successful. In succeeding rounds, more and more students will defect from the agreement, and the total payoff earned by the class will decrease rapidly.

DISCUSSION

Students who participate in this experiment have the opportunity to increase the total payoff of the entire class by engaging in collusive behavior. At the same time, individual students can increase their individual payoffs by defecting from any agreement to collude. Because this experiment places students in situations analogous to those faced by firms who are members of real-world cartels, it provides an excellent means of deepening their understanding of cartel behavior. It also provides a powerful antidote to their somewhat naive belief in the power of communication to solve the problems created by the strategic nature of this game. It drives home the fact that, in the absence of an external enforcement mechanism, agreements tend to break down whenever there is a significant benefit to be gained by those who defect.

QUESTIONS

1. What choice of strategies would have maximized the total payoff of the class?

   [The total payoff of the class is maximized if everyone in the class chooses "1" But any individual who chooses "0" will achieve a higher individual payoff.]

2. How much does the outcome of this game depend on whether players are allowed to communicate with each other?

   [Although communication may seem important in generating collusive behavior, it has little or no effect on the long-run outcome. Communication does nothing to alter the incentives created by the payoff structure of the game.]

REFERENCES/FURTHER READING

Bishop, Jerry E. "All for One...One for All? Don't Bet on It." Wall Street Journal (December 4, 1986): 37.

APPENDICES TO EXPERIMENT 10

- Student instructions
- Record sheet
- Decision sheets
- Transparency master

STUDENT INSTRUCTIONS

In this experiment, you will be called on to make a decision in each of a number of rounds. The object is to maximize your total earnings (that is, your total payoff) for all the rounds of the experiment.

In each round, you must enter your name, the round number, and your decision (either "0" or "1") on your record sheet and on one of the accompanying decision sheets. After decision sheets have been collected from all of the students in the class, the decisions will be tallied by the instructor and the number of students selecting "1" will be announced. Your earnings for the round will depend on your decision to select "0" or "1" *and* on the total number of students who selected "1" in that round (see the table on the attached page). You should then record the number of people who have selected "1," your earnings for the round, and your cumulative earnings.

The total number of rounds to be played in the experiment will be determined by the instructor. There is to be no talking during the exercise (except for questions you may have about the rules of the game).

Number of People Choosing "1"	Payoff for Those Choosing "1"	"0"
0	$ .00	$ .50
1	.04	.54
2	.08	.58
3	.12	.62
4	.16	.66
5	.20	.70
6	.24	.74
7	.28	.78
8	.32	.82
9	.36	.86
10	.40	.90
11	.44	.94
12	.48	.98
13	.52	1.02
14	.56	1.06
15	.60	1.10
16	.64	1.14
17	.68	1.18
18	.72	1.22
19	.76	1.26
20	.80	1.30
21	.84	1.34
22	.88	1.38
23	.92	1.42
24	.96	1.46
25	1.00	1.50
26	1.04	1.54
27	1.08	1.58
28	1.12	1.62
29	1.16	1.66
30	1.20	1.70

RECORD SHEET

NAME _____

Round	My "Decision" ("0" or "1")	Number of People Choosing #1	My Earnings This Period	My Cumulative Earnings
1	_____	_____	_____	_____
2	_____	_____	_____	_____
3	_____	_____	_____	_____
4	_____	_____	_____	_____
5	_____	_____	_____	_____
6	_____	_____	_____	_____
7	_____	_____	_____	_____
8	_____	_____	_____	_____
9	_____	_____	_____	_____
10	_____	_____	_____	_____
11	_____	_____	_____	_____
12	_____	_____	_____	_____

Oligopoly, Interdependence, & Collusion (I)

DECISION SHEET

Name _____

Round # _____

My decision is _____ (enter "0" or "1")

DECISION SHEET

Name _____

Round # _____

My decision is _____ (enter "0" or "1")

DECISION SHEET

Name _____

Round # _____

My decision is _____ (enter "0" or "1")

DECISION SHEET

Name _____

Round # _____

My decision is _____ (enter "0" or "1")

NO. OF PEOPLE CHOOSING NUMBER 1	PAYOFFS FOR THOSE WHO CHOOSE	
	#1	#0
0	$ .00	$ .50
1	.04	.54
2	.08	.58
3	.12	.62
4	.16	.66
5	.20	.70
6	.24	.74
7	.28	.78
8	.32	.82
9	.36	.86
10	.40	.90
11	.44	.94
12	.48	.98
13	.52	1.02
14	.56	1.06
15	.60	1.10
16	.64	1.14
17	.68	1.18
18	.72	1.22
19	.76	1.26
20	.80	1.30
21	.84	1.34
22	.88	1.38
23	.92	1.42
24	.96	1.46
25	1.00	1.50
26	1.04	1.54
27	1.08	1.58
28	1.12	1.62
29	1.16	1.66
30	1.20	1.70

EXPERIMENT 11: OLIGOPOLY, INTERDEPENDENCE, AND COLLUSION (II)

OVERVIEW

This experiment, like Experiment 10, demonstrates some of the problems inherent in maintaining collusive agreements under imperfectly competitive conditions. Students play a version of the repeated prisoner's dilemma in which the stakes are not jail time or corporate profits but the grade earned in the exercise.[1]

MATERIALS NEEDED

- Instructions and record sheets for distribution to the class

ADMINISTERING THE EXPERIMENT

Distribute the instructions and the record sheets to the class (both found in the Appendices at the end of this experiment). Read the instructions aloud, answering any questions about the mechanics of the game, but be certain not to discuss the advantages or disadvantages of any particular strategy. Also, be sure to emphasize to students that they are not to communicate with each other or with the instructor except for asking questions about the rules of the game.

The game consists of six rounds. In each round, each student plays the following game:

		"Rivals" Compete	Collude
You	Compete	10	40
	Collude	0	20

The object of the game is to maximize one's total payoff for the six rounds, because at the end of the game the payoff will be converted into a grade for the exercise according to the following scale: over 100 points.= A+; 90 - 100 points = A; 80 - 90 points = B; 70 - 80 points = C; 60 - 70 points = D; below 60 points = F. In each round, each student will decide to "compete" or "collude." To "compete," a student raises his or her open hand; to "collude," raises his or her fist. All hands are to be raised simultaneously on the count of three. The

---

[1] This experiment is adapted from Hemenway, Moore, and Whitney (1987).

response of the "Rivals" will be the strategy chosen by a majority of students in the class. At the end of each round, students record their payoffs on their record sheets. Give students a few moments to ponder their strategies for the next round, then repeat the same procedure for the next round. After the sixth round is completed, students sum their payoffs for all rounds and use this number to determine their grade for the exercise.

In most cases, a large majority of students in the class will vote to "compete" in each round, and the maximum score that any student receives for the game is 60 points.[2] When questioned about this result, students will generally be quick to point out that the uncertainty as to what the other members of the class will do, coupled with the inability of students to communicate with each other, is a major cause of their failure to achieve higher payoffs.

At this point, you can demonstrate your benevolence to the class by offering to discard the grades from the first game and giving them the opportunity to play the game again, this time after allowing them to discuss their strategies for a few minutes before the beginning of the first round and also briefly between rounds.

The discussion of strategy between students will usually result in an agreement to collude, since no student can achieve a grade higher than a "D" unless a majority of students choose to collude. During the initial rounds of the second game, a majority of students will usually choose to collude.[3] Those students who choose to collude will receive a payoff of 20 points, but those who choose to compete will receive a payoff of 40 points. By the fourth or fifth round (and sometimes earlier), the agreement to collude breaks down, and a majority of students choose to compete.

DISCUSSION

The following points are among those that Hemenway, Moore, and Whitney suggest be brought out after the exercise has been completed. First, the smaller the number of players in the game, the more likely it is that collusion will succeed. With a small number of players, the mutual interdependence of their decisions becomes more salient. Similarly, collusion is more likely to occur in industries in which there are a small number of firms. Second, communication is important in overcoming the incentive to compete. Without communication between the players, collusion is extremely unlikely. Third, collusion would be more likely to succeed if there were some device available to discipline defectors.

Hemenway, Moore, and Whitney also suggest two variations for the second game (that is, when communication is permitted). First, if the number of points necessary to achieve particular grades is increased, it may be possible for all students to achieve the highest grade only if designated students "cheat" in each round. For example, if the number of points required to achieve the grade of "A+" is increased to "over 120," then even unanimous collusion in all

---

[2] In Taylor's *Economics*, this solution is referred to as the "noncooperative outcome."

[3] This is the "cooperative outcome" described in Chapter 11 of Taylor's *Economics*.

six periods would result in each student receiving 120 points, one point shy of the number needed for an "A+." But all students could still receive grades of "A+" if a specific minority of students chose to "compete" in each round. This sort of collusive agreement turns out to be even more difficult to maintain, but, according to Hemenway, Moore, and Whitney, "the strategies, anxiety, and anger generated enrich the subsequent discussion of the outcome."[4]

As a second variation, Hemenway, et al. suggest that in the third or fourth round of the second game, students be informed that "because the antitrust authorities have become suspicious about the conduct of their industry," they will henceforth be required to decrease their level of communication by closing their eyes for the voting and vote counting during the remaining rounds. When communication is cut off in this manner, collusion tends to break down even more quickly.

QUESTIONS

1. Do you think that players in this game will be more or less likely to "collude" as the number of players in the game increases?

    [The likelihood of collusion decreases as the number of players increases. Larger groups tend to be less cohesive than small groups. Also, as the size of the group increases, it becomes more difficult to identify (and discipline?) defectors.]

2. How important is the ability to communicate in bringing about collusive behavior?

    [Without communication, large-scale collusive behavior is extremely unlikely. But even with communication, there is a powerful incentive to "compete" in this game.]

REFERENCES/FURTHER READING

Hemenway, David, Robert Moore, and James Whitney. "The Oligopoly Game." Economic Inquiry (October 1987): 727-730.

APPENDICES TO EXPERIMENT 11

- Instructions to hand out and/or read aloud before conducting the experiment
- Record sheets for students to record their decisions and their payoffs

---

[4]Every instructor must decide how much anxiety, anger, etc., he or she is willing to elicit in the name of illustrating an educational point. If you find yourself concerned over the possibility that the defectors in this experiment may suffer serious psychological damage as a result of the anger vented toward them by the other students, modify these procedures so that students indicate their decision to compete or collude anonymously by writing it on a simple form that they turn in to the instructor. Then tally the decisions for the round and inform the class how many students chose each option.

STUDENT INSTRUCTIONS

The following payoff matrix describes the game that you will be playing. The object of the game is to maximize your total "profits" (that is, your total payoff).

		"Rivals" Compete	Collude
You	Compete	10	40
	Collude	0	20

You will play this game for six rounds. In each round, you must decide whether to "compete" or "collude." Your payoff in each round will depend on the decision that you make, along with the decision made by the majority of your classmates. In each round, on the count of three, each student raises his or her hand, indicating "compete" by raising an open hand or "collude" by raising a fist. The response of your "rivals" will be the response of the majority of the students in the class.

Your payoff in each round will be as follows: if you choose to "compete," you earn 10 points if your "rivals" (that is, the majority of the class) also choose to "compete" and 40 points if your "rivals" choose to "collude." If you choose to "collude," you earn 0 points if your "rivals" choose to "compete" and 20 points if your "rivals" also choose to "collude." At the end of each period, enter your decision, your payoff for the period, and your cumulative payoff on the accompanying record sheet.

At the end of six rounds, you will receive a grade on this exercise that will be determined as follows: over 100 points = A+; 90 - 100 points = A; 80 - 90 points = B; 70 - 80 points = C; 60 - 70 points = D; below 60 points = F.

There is to be no talking during the exercise (except for questions you may have about the rules of the game).

At the end of the first game, the class will be given the option of playing the game a second time under slightly different rules.

Example: Suppose that, in the first round, more than half of you raise an open hand (that is, decide to "compete"). Then those of you who raised an open hand (that is, chose to "compete") would receive 10 points. Those of you who raised a fist (that is, chose to "collude") would receive 0 points. At that point, each student would record his or her decision and payoff on the record sheet. Also at that point, everyone would make a decision for the second round. Suppose that in the second round a majority of you raise a fist (that is, decide to "collude"). Then those of you who raised an open hand would receive 40 points and those of you who raised a fist would receive 20 points.

RECORD SHEET

NAME _____

GAME #1:

ROUND	MY DECISION	MY "RIVALS'" DECISION	MY EARNINGS	MY CUMULATIVE EARNINGS
1	_____	_____	_____	_____
2	_____	_____	_____	_____
3	_____	_____	_____	_____
4	_____	_____	_____	_____
5	_____	_____	_____	_____
6	_____	_____	_____	_____

GAME #2:

ROUND	MY DECISION	MY "RIVALS'" DECISION	MY EARNINGS	MY CUMULATIVE EARNINGS
1	_____	_____	_____	_____
2	_____	_____	_____	_____
3	_____	_____	_____	_____
4	_____	_____	_____	_____
5	_____	_____	_____	_____
6	_____	_____	_____	_____

EXPERIMENT 12: THE PRISONER'S DILEMMA

OVERVIEW

The prisoner's dilemma is a versatile model of strategic interaction; it can be used to illustrate the consequences of cooperative and noncooperative behavior in a wide variety of settings. The following experiment involves two firms engaged in a pricing game.[1]

MATERIALS NEEDED

- A blackboard (or overhead projector) to illustrate the payoff matrix

ADMINISTERING THE EXPERIMENT

Reproduce the payoff matrix from Figure 1 on the blackboard. Pair up students and assign each a role as either firm 1 or firm 2. Explain the nature of the payoff matrix to your students, noting that firm 1's payoff is in the upper right-hand corner of each box. Begin the experiment by asking each student to write down privately on a slip of paper his or her pricing strategy--either a high or a low price. Make sure that the students do not communicate with each other before recording their choices. After the pairs have made their choices, have them simultaneously reveal their choices to you and to each other so that they may calculate their payoffs.

Firm 1

		High Price	Low Price
Firm 2	High Price	500 / 500	700 / 50
	Low Price	50 / 700	200 / 200

Figure 1

DISCUSSION

Each "firm" has a dominant strategy in choosing a low price: no matter what choice the other player makes, a low price generates a larger payoff for each player. If each firm plays

---

[1]This experiment is adapted from Gardner (1995).

the dominant strategy of "low," the players arrive at what is called the noncooperative outcome--the lower right-hand box of the matrix--with each firm earning a payoff of 200.

On the other hand, if the players cooperate with each other, each firm receives a payoff of 700. The cooperative outcome, however, is not a stable equilibrium, since each player has an incentive to defect unilaterally (that is, to choose "low"). Consequently, the cooperative outcome is difficult to maintain and the players tend to arrive at the noncooperative outcome.

A number of variations of this game are possible. You could allow open communication among the students prior to their choice of strategies (but always require that choices be recorded privately on the slip of paper) so as to encourage cooperative behavior.

Another variation is designed to detect evidence of the unraveling phenomenon. Announce at the start of the experiment that you will play only five rounds. The unraveling phenomenon suggests that if a player knows that round 5 is the final round, he or she will have a powerful incentive to play noncooperatively (that is, to choose "low price") since there is no way for the other player to penalize him or her in subsequent rounds for defecting. If the other player also realizes this, he or she will also defect in the last round. By using backward induction, it can be shown that each player will also have an incentive to defect in rounds 4, 3, 2, and 1. Thus a series of repeated games with a known, finite number of rounds will "unravel" to a single-shot noncooperative outcome.

QUESTIONS

1. Under what circumstances is the cooperative outcome more likely?

    [The cooperative outcome is more likely to occur when the parties are able to freely communicate, when there is full information regarding payoffs, and when the game is played repeatedly.]

2. Design another example of a prisoner's dilemma game in a setting different from the pricing game just described.

    [This is up to the student's imagination.]

REFERENCES/FURTHER READING

Gardner, Roy. Games For Business and Economics. John Wiley & Sons, Inc., 1995.

APPENDIX TO EXPERIMENT 12

- Payoff matrix

PAYOFF MATRIX

Firm 1

		High Price	Low Price
Firm 2	High Price	500 / 500	700 / 50
	Low Price	50 / 700	200 / 200

Note: Firm 1's payoff is located in the upper right-hand corner of each box.

EXPERIMENT 13: AN EXPERIMENTAL TEST OF PREFERENCES OVER THE DISTRIBUTION OF INCOME

OVERVIEW

This exercise investigates the question of how much income distribution individuals desire in a society with random differences in individual incomes.[1] Individuals are confronted with choices among lotteries that determine their own payoffs--to determine their individual levels of risk aversion--and with choices among lotteries that determine the payoffs of everyone in a larger group--to determine their preferences regarding the distribution of income within a larger group.

MATERIALS NEEDED

- Student handouts
- A die

ADMINISTERING THE EXPERIMENT

This exercise consists of three parts.[2] In part A, each student's payoff is determined individually in the following manner. First, each student (privately) selects a particular row (that is, A through O) from a table (see Table 1) that appears in the student handout (found in the Appendix at the end of this experiment). After all students have made their selections and turned in their forms, a single die is rolled. If the die shows 1, 3, or 5, each student receives the amount in the column headed "odd" from the row which they have previously selected. If the die shows 2, 4, or 6, each student receives the amount in the column headed "even" from the row they previously selected.

In part B of the exercise, each student's payoff is again determined by a separate roll of the die for each student. Each student selects a particular row from Table 1, but this time with the understanding that one randomly selected student's form will be used to determine the

---

[1] This is an edited version of an experiment that John Beck contributed to the Spring, 1992, issue of *Classroom Expernomics*.

[2] In the original research design, one of these three parts was randomly selected at the end of the experiment and students received only the payoff they had earned for that part. This was a way to keep down the total cost of payments to subjects while maintaining their incentives to maximize their payoffs in each part of the exercise. In a classroom setting, where payments are made in bonus points (or not at all), this particular aspect of the exercise can be dropped.

payoffs of each individual in the class.[3] After all the students have turned in their forms, one form is drawn at random. Each student's payoff is then determined by a separate roll of the die.

	Odd	Even
A	$25.00	$0.00
B	$23.05	$1.15
C	$21.20	$2.20
D	$19.45	$3.15
E	$17.80	$4.00
F	$16.25	$4.75
G	$14.80	$5.40
H	$13.45	$5.95
I	$12.20	$6.40
J	$11.05	$6.75
K	$10.00	$7.00
L	$ 9.05	$7.15
M	$ 8.20	$7.20
N	$ 7.45	$7.15
O	$ 7.08	$7.08

Table 1

In part C, each student's payoff is again determined by a separate roll of the die. But students must unanimously agree on which row will be used to determine the payoffs of everyone in the class.[4] If the group does not reach a unanimous agreement in a specified amount of time,[5] then the payoff for each student in the class will be zero.

DISCUSSION

This experiment can provide significant insights into students' preferences over various distributions of income. Since students must make their choice over income distributions without knowing where their individual incomes will fall in the distribution (that is, "even" or "odd"), they are operating behind a "veil of ignorance" akin to that contemplated by Rawls. Under these circumstances, students can be expected to reveal their actual preference over various distributional states rather than favor rules that give them some advantage at the expense of other

---

[3] And also with the understanding that no portion of the payoffs may be transferred between students after the experiment. If payments are made in cash, of course, this rule is unenforceable. If payments are made in the form of bonus points (or not at all), such transfers are not possible.

[4] And again, post-experiment transfers are prohibited.

[5] Beck suggests fifteen minutes.

members of society. In part A, since each student's selection affects only the probability distribution from which his or her individual income is drawn, students' choices can be viewed as measuring their levels of risk aversion. In Table 1, income distribution A has the highest mean value, $12.50. One would expect risk-averse individuals to select an income distribution with a lower expected mean, but with less inequality. Only extremely risk-averse individuals (that is, those using the Rawlsian maximin criterion) would select distribution M. If individuals are risk averse, then that fact might provide a rationale for some degree of income redistribution based on an "insurance motive"--that is, individuals who are uncertain about their position in the income distribution might prefer some reduction in inequality even if it reduces the mean expected income.

In part B of the experiment, since each student is selecting a lottery that will be used to determine not only his or her own payoff but also that of every other individual in the class, students' choices can be viewed as revealing their preferences regarding differences in income within the group. These choices can be compared with their choices in part A to determine whether students' preferences over the distribution of income within the group (*not* just their individual risk aversion) are part of their motive for favoring income distribution. That is, if students' choices in part B are more egalitarian than their choices in part A, it implies that something beyond their individual risk aversion is at work in their choice of income distributions.

Rawls's theory of justice is a contractarian theory in that the criteria for justice are rules people would hypothetically unanimously adopt in an "original position" in which individuals do not know what their positions in society will be. Part C of the experiment is similar to part B except for the requirement that the members of the group *unanimously* agree to adopt a particular income distribution. This part of the experiment is intended to examine Rawls's conjecture that individuals in this position would adopt a maximin rule.

This experiment is designed less to illustrate economic theory than to allow students to examine their own revealed preferences in light of economic theory. Although the results may vary from one group of students to another, Beck [1992] advises us to expect this experiment to reveal that 1) students are risk averse, but 2) they do not display the extreme risk aversion implied by a Rawlsian maximin rule.

QUESTIONS

1. Calculate the expected payoff associated with each of the lotteries (that is, A through O) in the table.

    [Since the probability of receiving either the "odd" or the "even" payoff is .5, the expected payoff of any lottery is equal to the average of the two payoffs.]

2. Which lottery has the highest expected value? What are the implications of an individual selecting a lottery with a lower expected value in part A of the experiment?

[Lottery A has the highest expected value, $12.50. Individuals who select lotteries with lower expected values might do so because they are risk averse.]

REFERENCES/FURTHER READING

Beck, John H. "An Experimental Test of Preferences for the Distribution of Income." Classroom Expernomics (Spring 1992): 2-3.

APPENDIX TO EXPERIMENT 13

- Student handout

STUDENT HANDOUT

This experiment consists of three parts, A, B, and C. At the end of the experiment, there will be a random drawing to determine which part will be used to determine your individual payoffs.

PART A

If part A is used, your payoff will be determined by the roll of a die at the end of the period. If the die shows 1, 3, or 5, you will receive the amount in the column headed "odd"; if the die shows 2, 4, or 6, you will receive the amount shown in the column headed "even." Payoffs will be made privately, so you will know only your own payoff. You must choose which row in the table--A, B, C, etc.--will be used to determine your payoff.

	Odd	Even
A	$25.00	$0.00
B	$23.05	$1.15
C	$21.20	$2.20
D	$19.45	$3.15
E	$17.80	$4.00
F	$16.25	$4.75
G	$14.80	$5.40
H	$13.45	$5.95
I	$12.20	$6.40
J	$11.05	$6.75
K	$10.00	$7.00
L	$ 9.05	$7.15
M	$ 8.20	$7.20
N	$ 7.45	$7.15
O	$ 7.08	$7.08

Fill in your name and circle the letter of the row that you want to determine your payoff.

Name _____

PART B

In this part of the experiment, your payoff will also be determined by the roll of a die at the end of the experiment according to the same schedule used in part A, which is reproduced below. If the die shows 1, 3, or 5, you will receive the amount in the column headed "odd"; if the die shows 2, 4, or 6, you will receive the amount shown in the column headed "even." The die will be rolled separately for each individual in the class. Payoffs will be made publicly, so everyone will know how much everyone else receives. Unlike part A, however, each individual will not be able to choose a different row to determine the payoff. Each of you must choose which row in the table--A, B, C, etc.--you want to be used to determine the payoffs for *everyone* in the class. Before throwing the die to determine individual payoffs, one of these forms will be drawn at random; the row designated on that form will be used to determine individual payoffs for all students in the class. You are not allowed to make any transfers of part of your payoff to other students in the class after the experiment has concluded.

	Odd	Even
A	$25.00	$0.00
B	$23.05	$1.15
C	$21.20	$2.20
D	$19.45	$3.15
E	$17.80	$4.00
F	$16.25	$4.75
G	$14.80	$5.40
H	$13.45	$5.95
I	$12.20	$6.40
J	$11.05	$6.75
K	$10.00	$7.00
L	$ 9.05	$7.15
M	$ 8.20	$7.20
N	$ 7.45	$7.15
O	$ 7.08	$7.08

Fill in your name and circle the letter of the row that you want to determine the payoffs for all members of the class.

Name _____

EXPERIMENT 14: A PUBLIC GOODS EXPERIMENT

OVERVIEW

This experiment illustrates the nature and extent of free-riding behavior in the provision of a public good.[1] The clash between private and social returns is clearly demonstrated through the use of a voluntary contribution mechanism.

MATERIALS NEEDED

- Decision forms and record sheets
- A blackboard to record each period's results

ADMINISTERING THE EXPERIMENT

This experiment utilizes a voluntary contribution mechanism that allows students (or teams of students) to make investment decisions in which they must allocate an endowment of "tokens" into either of two accounts: a private account or a group account. Each token invested in the private account generates a return of $.20 for the individual investor. Each token invested in the group account generates a return of $.50, which is then shared by all investors in the group--whether or not they contributed to the group account. The team share generated by contributions to the group account is $(\$.50)G/N$ where G is the sum of all team contributions to the group account in any given period and N is the number of investors (or teams of investors). Note that although each investor's marginal per capita return on the private account is $.20, each investor's marginal per capita return from the group account is $(\$.50)/N$. Since the marginal per capita return on the private account exceeds that of the group account (for an appropriately chosen value of N), the dominant individual strategy is to contribute all tokens to the private account, even though all investors would be better off if everyone contributed to the group account. A payoff table (found in the Appendices which follow) indicates the payoffs for various levels of contribution to the group account.

In preparation for the experiment, decide on the number of teams, periods, and tokens in each team's endowment in order to generate a representative payoff table and to make sure that you have an adequate number of record sheets and decision forms. At the beginning of the class, divide the students into teams and pass out all materials. Review the instructions orally (perhaps using an overhead transparency) to generate common information and answer any questions. Include an explanation of the reward system at this time.

---

[1] This experiment is adapted from Brock (1991).

PART C

In this part of the experiment, your payoff will be determined by another roll of the die at the end of the experiment according to the same schedule used in part A, which is reproduced below. If the die shows 1, 3, or 5, you will receive the amount in the column headed "odd"; if the die shows 2, 4, or 6, you will receive the amount shown in the column headed "even." The die will be rolled separately for each individual in the class. Payoffs will be made publicly, so everyone will know how much everyone else receives. Unlike part A, however, each individual will not be able to choose a different row to determine the payoff. The entire group must unanimously agree on which row in the table--A, B, C, etc.--will be used to determine the payoffs for everyone in the class. If the group does not reach unanimous agreement within fifteen minutes, the payoffs from part C will be zero. You are not allowed to make any transfers of part of your payoff to other students in the class after the experiment is concluded.

	Odd	Even
A	$25.00	$0.00
B	$23.05	$1.15
C	$21.20	$2.20
D	$19.45	$3.15
E	$17.80	$4.00
F	$16.25	$4.75
G	$14.80	$5.40
H	$13.45	$5.95
I	$12.20	$6.40
J	$11.05	$6.75
K	$10.00	$7.00
L	$ 9.05	$7.15
M	$ 8.20	$7.20
N	$ 7.45	$7.15
O	$ 7.08	$7.08

Begin the first period by asking the teams to make their allocation decisions on the decision forms. Collect the forms and total the contributions to the group account in order to calculate the team share from the group account. Report both the total contributions and the team share to the class by recording the information on the blackboard. Finally, ask the teams to tally up their earnings on their record sheets, reminding them that everyone earned the same team share from the group account. Repeat this procedure for every period.

As a variation on the experiment, you may want to allow the teams to "collude" after a few periods. Indeed, once students become frustrated with the relatively low earnings generated in the early periods, they may request that communication across teams be permitted. The instructor can accommodate this demand simply by leaving the room for a few minutes, during which the students are free to discuss whatever they want. Upon the instructor's return, the teams are then given the opportunity to complete their decision forms privately.

DISCUSSION

After completing the predetermined number of decision periods and providing you have enough time remaining in the class, you may wish to begin your debriefing session immediately. First of all, begin with a plot of the contributions to the group account as a share of all tokens over each period. Figure 1 illustrates the results of a typical experiment.[2] The number of tokens invested in the group account will generally be 30 to 60 percent of the total possible in the first round and decline each round until collusion is permitted (period 4 in this example). Although collusion should increase investment in the public good, a significant underinvestment is still likely.

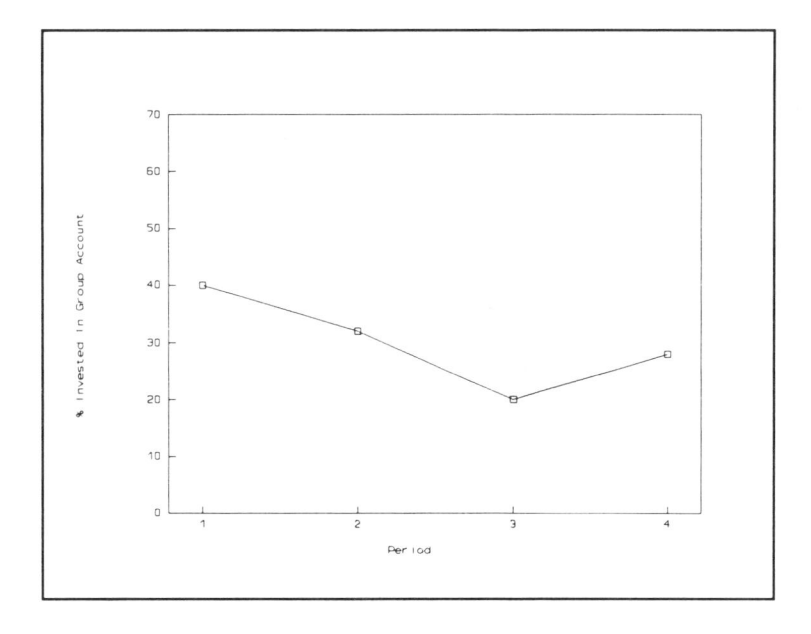

Figure 1

---

[2]Figure 1 is from Brock (1991).

Besides allowing communication, additional variations affecting the rate of free riding involve manipulating the returns to the private and group accounts, and changing the number of teams.

QUESTIONS

1. What impact would an increase in the number of teams have on the free-rider phenomenon? Explain.

   [While conventional wisdom would suggest that free riding should increase as the group size increases, experiments conducted by Isaac and Walker (1988) indicate just the opposite: increases in group size lead to larger contribution rates to the group account.]

2. How is the structure of this experiment similar to that of the prisoner's dilemma?

   [The voluntary contribution game is identical to the prisoner's dilemma. Each participant has two strategies: contribute or don't contribute to the group account. The cooperative (maximum joint payoff) outcome is for all participants to contribute all tokens to the group account.]

REFERENCES/FURTHER READING

Brock, John R. "A Public Goods Experiment for the Classroom." Economic Inquiry (April 1991): 395-401.

Leuthold, Jane H. "A Free-Rider Experiment for the Large Class." Journal of Economic Education (Fall 1993): 353-363.

Williams, Arlington W., and James M. Walker. "Computerized Laboratory Exercises for Microeconomics Education: Three Applications Motivated by Experimental Economics." Journal of Economic Education (Fall 1993): 291-315.

APPENDICES TO EXPERIMENT 14

- Student instructions
- Decision forms
- Payoff table
- Transparency master (payoff table)

STUDENT INSTRUCTIONS

This is an experiment in the economics of group decision making. The class will be divided into ____ teams (each composed of one or more members). The experiment will occur over a sequence of ____ decision-making periods. At the start of every period, each team will be endowed with ____ tokens. In each period, each team must invest its endowed tokens in either a private account or a group account. Each team in the class has its own private account, but there is only one group account for the entire class.

Each team will earn $.20 for each token that is placed in the private account. Each token placed in the group account will generate earnings of $.50 for the entire class. The earnings from the group account will be divided equally among all teams, regardless of the number of tokens that any individual team places in the group account.

You may not communicate with any other team without the permission of the instructor.

Round	Team Share of Earnings from Group Account	Total Earnings from Private Account	Total Earned by Period	Cumulative Earnings

DECISION FORMS

```
Team: _____        Round: _____
Token allotment: _____

Decision:

1.  Invest in private account: _____ tokens
2.  Invest in group account:   _____ tokens
```

```
Team: _____        Round: _____
Token allotment: _____

Decision:

1.  Invest in private account: _____ tokens
2.  Invest in group account:   _____ tokens
```

```
Team: _____        Round: _____
Token allotment: _____

Decision:

1.  Invest in private account: _____ tokens
2.  Invest in group account:   _____ tokens
```

```
Team: _____        Round: _____
Token allotment: _____

Decision:

1.  Invest in private account: _____ tokens
2.  Invest in group account:   _____ tokens
```

PAYOFF TABLE

Total Tokens Invested in Group Account	Total Group Earnings	Team Share of Group Earnings
0	0.00	0.00
50	25.00	1.25
100	50.00	2.50
150	75.00	3.75
200	100.00	5.00
250	125.00	6.25
300	150.00	7.50
350	175.00	8.75
400	200.00	10.00
450	225.00	11.25
500	250.00	12.50

PAYOFF TABLE

Total Tokens Invested in Group Account	Total Group Earnings	Team Share of Group Earnings
0	0.00	0.00
50	25.00	1.25
100	50.00	2.50
150	75.00	3.75
200	100.00	5.00
250	125.00	6.25
300	150.00	7.50
350	175.00	8.75
400	200.00	10.00
450	225.00	11.25
500	250.00	12.50

EXPERIMENT 15: A POLLUTION RIGHTS TRADING GAME

OVERVIEW

The Environmental Protection Agency (EPA) has in recent years moved toward market-based incentives as an alternative to command-and-control measures to achieve pollution reduction. A limited pollution rights market has existed since 1976, but a higher level of activity is occurring in response to Title IV of the 1990 Clean Air Act Amendments. Beginning in 1995, fossil fuel power plants nationwide are being forced to cut sulfur dioxide (SO_2) emissions by 40 percent through market incentives provided by the EPA. The goal is to allow the industry to choose least-cost emission reduction rather than using across-the-board mandates that limit emissions or require specific technology.

The following classroom game allows students to determine the best choice among alternatives for meeting a regulatory goal of reduced emissions.[1] Acting as the managers of several different industries, students can compare the cost of pollution reduction to the cost of acquiring permits to pollute. The appeal of the game is that students who often have trouble accepting the concept of pollution rights have no trouble using market forces to allocate them efficiently.

MATERIALS NEEDED

- A student worksheet to assist students in calculating the costs of alternative approaches of pollution control for each industry in the market
- A record of transactions to assist students in describing how they complied with EPA standards
- Mock certificates representing emission permits

ADMINISTERING THE EXPERIMENT

Begin by discussing with students the concept of regulatory control over air emissions and the differences between command and market-based incentive methods of regulating. The key ideas for the students to consider are the regulatory agency's goal of reducing pollution emissions and the companies' goal of minimizing the costs of any pollution reduction they are forced to do. The attractive feature of the tradable emission rights, compared to command-and-control, is that both goals can be achieved at a lower opportunity cost to society.

---

[1] This experiment is the work of Rachel Nugent of Pacific Lutheran University. It has been edited to fit our format.

Begin the game by dividing the class into several small groups, which allows several industries or plants to be established. In order for emissions permits to be profitably traded, eligible companies or plants must face different costs of pollution abatement. This can be done in the classroom either by creating different industries, each of which emits a selected pollutant, or by creating plants within the same industry that use different production technologies. In this case you can create plants of various ages each operating with a different cost structure. In the current version of the experiment, there are several different polluting industries. This emphasizes the fact that even apparently "clean" industries do pollute and that society benefits from emissions reduction regardless of the specific identity of the polluter.

Each small group in the classroom (two students per group is a minimum number that allows a "manager" and a "trader" for each company) represents a company within an industry that is emitting a specific pollutant (use only one type of pollutant for simplicity). Each company faces a different schedule of pollution-abatement costs, based on its product and technology. Again for simplicity, a constant marginal cost of abatement schedule is used. In more advanced classes, the marginal cost of abatement could be rising as emissions are reduced. Finally, each company is given a simple formula relating profit levels to output.

In the first stage of the exercise, small groups complete the top portion of the student worksheet (found in the Appendices at the end of this experiment) for their respective companies. In this step, students recognize the relationship between their emissions and output levels, and their output levels and profit levels. Using these simple linear relationships, they calculate their company's total current emissions and current profits. Each company is producing some pollution in the production process. Students can recognize at this stage that pollution reduction will not be obtained in a costless manner. They should be able to remember (or can be reminded) that if firms are already profit-maximizing, pollution abatement will impose costs, and it is their responsibility to achieve it in the least-cost manner. This condition is combined in the next step with differing costs of cleanup to create the opportunity for profitable trades among the companies.

Stage 2 begins with the regulatory agency (the instructor) imposing an emissions limit which mandates a 50 percent overall reduction in emissions. Although the initial allocation of pollution rights is an important equity issue in real-life regulatory discussions, it is avoided in this exercise. Thus, the 50 percent emissions reduction is imposed on each firm, which will reveal to each student group the amount of emissions reduction it must achieve. The environmental regulator (again, the instructor) distributes a predetermined number of emissions permits equally to the companies as indicated on the student worksheet (found in the Appendices at the end of this experiment). It is useful to have both 1-ton and 5-ton permits available for the exercise.

Compliance can be accomplished in a variety of ways, and each group of students should now complete the remainder of the student worksheet for its company. This requires the company groups to calculate the costs of each of their available options. Some industries will have excess pollution rights, while some will have insufficient pollution permits to meet their new requirement. Their choices are to install cleaning equipment, reduce output (and thereby associated emissions), or acquire sufficient pollution rights. Once the costs of choosing each of these compliance methods are evident, students will determine their company's optimal decision and permit trading can begin. The students are given a limited amount of time to balance their actual emission levels with their allowable emission levels. They will seek to achieve the required emissions level in the least-cost way. If they do not meet their mandatory limit, the environmental regulator will shut them down and they will lose all profits (or suffer losses equal to fixed costs) in the next time period.

An equilibrium price will be established for the pollution rights. Depending on how much time students have for trading (and the initial conditions), there may be some dispersion in transaction prices as it takes some practice for them to become savvy market participants. In order to allow students to learn the concept well, and to allow for some of the extensions described in the next section, several permit trading sessions can be run before the results are discussed.

DISCUSSION

The student groups will find that each industry faces different incentives to trade. The software industry will have excess permits, but facing a high marginal cleanup cost will retain one permit in order to meet its emission reduction requirement. The pulp and coal industries are relatively "dirty" and will be forced to clean up or reduce output, but will also trade permits depending on the price because of their relatively low marginal cleanup costs. The steel mill faces a higher marginal cleanup cost and doesn't require much emission reduction. It will keep its allocation of permits and purchase an additional number to meet its mandate.

Because of the disparities among the industries, the equilibrium price is dependent on the nature of trades among the groups. It is possible that the student groups will not achieve one equilibrium price, but may trade permits at several prices. This situation will not interfere with the main point of the game and, in fact, can provide an opportunity to discuss the advantages of more players in providing an efficiently functioning market. The expected results of the trading process are noted in the student worksheet answer key in the "best choice" row.

There are many aspects of this exercise that lend themselves to productive classroom discussion. The most important of these is the idea that market-based incentives are a more efficient way to achieve pollution cleanup than command-and-control methods. Thus, students have been asked to complete the student worksheet in order to highlight this result. They will find that pollution cleanup lowers profits across the board (as the companies were all assumed to be profit maximizers prior to the regulation), but by less than if they all were forced to use cleanup technology to meet emissions goals. They will also find that the companies reduced emissions by different proportions, even though the regulatory mandate initially imposed equiproportional reductions on each of them. Discussing this result will again emphasize that it is efficient for society to have cleanup performed in the lowest-cost manner.

This can lead into a discussion of some of the equity issues raised by market-based emissions permits. Among these are the initial allocation of permits, the issue of a "right to pollute," and ability to pay. Students can be asked to argue for different allocation schemes and explore the welfare consequences of granting more pollution rights to bigger polluters (enshrining the status quo and providing windfall benefits to existing firms) versus treating all firms or plants within an industry equally (potentially leading to major transitional costs or shutting down large polluters). This issue of a "right to pollute" can be quite contentious and, if the class is concerned about this aspect or the instructor wishes to explore the ethical questions, a good discussion can result.

Class discussion should emphasize that achieving pollution reduction more efficiently is not antithetical to--and is more likely to achieve--greater pollution reduction. One interesting extension of the game is the creation of an environmental organization that is allowed to purchase emission permits with funds raised from membership fees. The class can demonstrate its willingness to pay for environmental protection in that manner. Each student can be asked how much he or she would contribute to an environmental organization dedicated to air pollution reduction, and a group can be formed to represent these environmental interests. This group can then join in the emissions trading market. It can be interesting to see whether students respond with a different willingness to pay for the environmental activity when they realize their companies will face higher abatement costs as permits become more scarce.

QUESTIONS

1. How well do you think the process of permit trading would work in the real world?

2. What are some possible problems with this approach?

3. Does this approach provide an incentive for companies to reduce their emissions by more than the minimum required amounts?

   [Yes. If a company can reduce its emissions at a cost which is less than the going price of a pollution permit, the company will find it is to their advantage to reduce its emissions and sell any excess permits at the higher price, thereby raising its profits.]

4. What would happen in the trading process if the environmental regulator decided to reduce emissions even further?

   [The demand for pollution permits would increase and the market price of permits would rise.]

5. What would happen in the trading process if cleanup technology improved and the cost of cleanup equipment dropped?

   [The demand for pollution permits would decrease and the market price of permits would fall.]

REFERENCES/FURTHER READING

Field, Barry C. Environmental Economics. McGraw-Hill, 1994.

Passell, Peter. "Cheapest Protection of Nature May Lie in Taxes, Not Laws." New York Times (November 24, 1994): B5.

Taylor, Jeffrey. "New Rules Harness Power of Free Markets to Curb Air Pollution." Wall Street Journal (April 14, 1992): A1.

Tietenberg, Tom. Emissions Trading. Johns Hopkins University Press for Resources for the Future, 1985.

APPENDICES TO EXPERIMENT 15

- Student worksheet (to be completed by students)
- Student worksheet (answer key)
- Record of transactions (to be completed by students)

STUDENT WORKSHEET

OUTPUT, EMISSIONS, AND PROFITS OF VARIOUS INDUSTRIES

	Software	Pulp Mill	Steel Mill	Coal Plant
Current Output	20Q	1000Q	100Q	1,000Q
Current Emissions (E=f(Q))	.1 ton/Q	.5 ton/Q	.3 ton/Q	1 ton/Q
Total Emissions (tons)				
Profits (π=f(Q))	$10,000*Q	$1,000*Q	$1,000*Q	$100*Q
Total Profits ($)				

COSTS OF CLEANUP OPTIONS FOR VARIOUS INDUSTRIES

	Software	Pulp Mill	Steel Mill	Coal Plant
Emission Limit	1 ton	250 tons	15 tons	500 tons
Emissions Reduction Required				
Permits Allocated	10 tons	10 tons	10 tons	10 tons
Cost of Cleanup (per ton of emissions)	$50,000/ton	$1,000/ton	$2,000/ton	$500/ton
Cost of Cleanup to required Level of Emissions				
Opportunity Cost of Reducing Output to Required Level of Emissions				
Permits Traded				
Best Choice and Effect on Profits				

Pollution Rights Trading Game

OUTPUT, EMISSIONS, AND PROFITS OF VARIOUS INDUSTRIES

	Software	Pulp Mill	Steel Mill	Coal Plant
Current Output	20Q	1000Q	100Q	1,000Q
Current Emissions (E=f(Q))	.1 ton/Q	.5 ton/Q	.3 ton/Q	1 ton/Q
Total Emissions (tons)	*2 tons*	*500 tons*	*30 tons*	*1,000 tons*
Profits (π=f(Q))	$10,000*Q	$1,000*Q	$1,000*Q	$100*Q
Total Profits ($)	*$200,000*	*$1,000,000*	*$100,000*	*$100,000*

COSTS OF CLEANUP OPTIONS FOR VARIOUS INDUSTRIES

	Software	Pulp Mill	Steel Mill	Coal Plant
Emission Limit	1 ton	250 tons	15 tons	500 tons
Emissions Reduction Required	*1 ton*	*250 tons*	*15 tons*	*500 tons*
Permits Allocated	10 tons	10 tons	10 tons	10 tons
Cost of Cleanup (per ton of emissions)	$50,000/ton	$1,000/ton	$2,000/ton	$500/ton
Cost of Cleanup to required Level of Emissions	$50,000	$250,000	$30,000	$250,000
Opportunity Cost of Reducing Output to Required Level of Emissions	$100,000	$500,000	$50,000	$50,000
Permits Traded	*Use 1, Sell 9*	*Buy 14*	*Buy 5*	*Sell 10*
Best Choice and Effect on Profits	*Clean no emissions, retain 1 permit, sell 9 permits @ up to $2,000 each. $\Delta\pi \leq \$18,000$*	*Clean 236 tons at $1,000 and buy 14 tons of permits @ up to $1,000 each. $\Delta\pi \leq -\$250,000$*	*Clean no emissions, retain 10 tons of permits, and buy 5 tons of permits @ up to $2,000. $\Delta\pi \leq -\$10,000$*	*Clean 500 tons of emissions at $100 each and sell 10 permits for at least $1,000 each. $\Delta\pi \leq -\$40,000$*

The italicized data is to be completed by students. It is provided here for the instructor's convenience.

RECORD OF TRANSACTIONS

1. Which company do you represent?

2. How many permits did you keep?

3. How many permits did you sell?

4. If you sold permits, what price(s) did you receive for your permits?

5. What was the total amount your company received for selling permits?

6. If your company bought permits, what price(s) did you pay for the permits?

7. What was the total amount your company spent on permits?

8. Did your company install pollution cleanup technology?

9. If so, how much did you spend on cleanup?

10. What were your company's total annual profits after compliance with the pollution regulations? (Hint: Calculate current profits minus cleanup expenses plus revenues from permit sales minus payments to obtain permits.)

11. How much did this process increase or decrease your company's profits?

12. How much did your company save compared to a scenario where the only choice was to install pollution cleanup technology? (Hint: Calculate cleanup costs minus "best choice" costs.)

13. Was your company able to meet its pollution abatement requirement?

14. What percentage of your emissions was eliminated?

15. How would the environmental regulator enforce compliance with these standards?

EXPERIMENT 16: THE COASE THEOREM

OVERVIEW

The following experiment effectively demonstrates the Coase theorem's remarkable conclusion that parties engaged in a dispute involving externalities can achieve a Pareto optimal outcome through bilateral bargaining.[1] Student pairs must make a joint decision on the level of some activity where the payoffs to each party are inversely correlated and only one activity level maximizes the joint payoff.

MATERIALS NEEDED

- Instructions, agreement forms, and payoff tables to distribute to students
- A fair coin for determining "controller" status

ADMINISTERING THE EXPERIMENT

To begin the experiment, pair up your students and randomly assign the letters A and B to each pair. Distribute a copy of the instructions and a payoff table to each student and an agreement form to each pair of students (see the Appendices at the end of this experiment). After reviewing the instructions with the students, conduct a coin flip to determine which member of each pair will be the "controller." Instruct the pairs to begin the experiment.

The pairs should participate together in choosing a number from a given set of numbers. The value of each number to each student is listed in Table 1. Note that the students' payoffs are negatively correlated. One of the students in each pair will be designated the "controller." The controller may, if he or she wishes, choose the number by himself or herself and inform the instructor, who will stop the experiment and pay both participants. The other participant may attempt to influence the controller to reach a mutually acceptable joint decision; the other participant may offer to pay part or all of his or her earnings to the controller.

If a joint agreement is reached, both parties must sign the agreement form, stating both what the chosen number will be and how much money will be transferred from one participant to the other. If a joint agreement is reached and the form is signed, the instructor will terminate the experiment and pay each participant according to the terms set forth in the agreement.

Repeat the experiment (with or without any changes in conditions) as time permits.

---

[1] This experiment is adapted from Hoffman and Spitzer (1982).

Number	A	B
0	0.00	12.00
1	4.00	10.00
2	6.00	6.00
3	8.00	4.00
4	9.00	2.00
5	10.00	1.00
6	11.00	0.00

Table 1

DISCUSSION

The instructions tell the students to choose one of a given set of numbers and that they will be paid different amounts of money depending on which number is chosen. As Hoffman and Spitzer (1982) describe it:

> In this formulation, the numbers are analogous to the productive decisions in the Coase theorem. For example, subjects A and B might correspond to the adjacent rancher and farmer in Coase's original model. Similarly, the chosen numbers might correspond to the size of the rancher's herd, and the money that was paid to the subjects might represent the rancher's and farmer's profits. The students were told that one of them had the power to choose the number unilaterally. This power is analogous to a property right in the Coase situation. For example, the controller's ability to choose the number might correspond to the farmer's right to obtain an injunction preventing the rancher from allowing his cows to wander onto the farmer's land. (Hoffman and Spitzer, 1982, pp. 84-85)

Thus, the instructions attempt to capture the base essentials for the Coase theorem to hold: two parties who are fully informed about each other's payoffs and who have no transaction costs to worry about. Furthermore, side payments are allowed and all contracts are in writing and strictly enforced.

For representative results, consider Table 2, which depicts the results of one experiment. The joint maximum was achieved by eleven of twelve bargaining pairs--which may be interpreted as evidence in support of the Coase theorem. Controllers tended either to split the profits equally with the other participant or to pursue the individual maxima. The incidence of the equal-split outcome is surprising in light of the individual rationality property of game theoretic models, but it is in line with results of some social psychology experiments that do not instruct subjects to be individually rational.

The Coase Theorem

Number of Pairs	Joint Maximum, Pareto Optimal	Equal Splits (or within $1 of equality)	Controller Individually Rational
12	11	5	7

Table 2[2]

QUESTIONS

1. Speculate as to what bargaining conditions are more likely to generate equal splits of the profits.

   [Equal splits are more likely to occur among bargaining pairs when 1) there is complete information about each other's payoffs and 2) the parties play the game repeatedly with each other.]

2. To what extent does the incidence of equal splits of the profits contradict the Coase theorem?

   [Since the controller can always obtain a larger payoff compared to the equal split outcome, the incidence of equal splits seems to contradict the rationality assumption. The "focalness" of the equal split outcome may be due to the bargainers' perceptions of fairness--that is, whether the right to be the controller was "earned."]

REFERENCES/FURTHER READING

Hoffman, Elizabeth, and Matthew Spitzer. "The Coase Theorem: Some Experimental Tests." Journal of Law and Economics (1982): 73-98.

APPENDICES TO EXPERIMENT 16

- Student instructions
- Payoff table and agreement form

---

[2] This table is taken from Hoffman and Spitzer (1982).

STUDENT INSTRUCTIONS

You are about to participate in an experiment in decision making. The purpose of the experiment is to gain insight into certain features of complex economic processes.

You will be asked to make several choices. Each choice will involve choosing a number. The cash value of the number to you is given in the set of payoff sheets attached to your instructions. For example, if $5 were next to number 2 on your payoff sheet and if number 2 were chosen, then you would be paid $5. In the following example, for instance, you might be person B. Your payoff sheets list not only the value of each number to you, but also the value of each number to the other participant.

Two of you will participate together on each decision. One of you will be designated the "controller." The controller may, if he or she wishes, choose the number by himself or herself and inform the monitor, who will stop the experiment and pay both participants. The other participant may attempt to influence the controller to reach a mutually acceptable joint decision; the other participant may offer to pay part or all of his or her earnings to the controller.

Example: Assume that A is the controller and that participants A and B have the following payoffs associated with numbers 0, 1, and 2:

Number	A's Payoff ($)	B's Payoff ($)
0	4	1
1	5	2
2	3	5

If A and B were to agree to set the number at 0, and further agree that B should get $1 from A's payoff, then the monitor would terminate the experiment, pay A $3 (representing the $4 payoff less the $1 transfer to B) and pay B $2 (representing the $1 payoff plus the $1 transfer from A).

If a joint agreement is reached, both parties must sign the attached agreement form, stating both what the chosen number will be and how much money will be transferred from one participant to the other. *No physical threats are allowed.* If a joint agreement is made and the form is signed, the monitor will terminate the experiment and pay each participant according to the terms set forth in the agreement.

Are there any questions?

PAYOFF TABLE

Number	A's Payoff	B's Payoff
0	$ 0.00	$12.00
1	4.00	10.00
2	6.00	6.00
3	8.00	4.00
4	9.00	2.00
5	10.00	1.00
6	11.00	0.00

AGREEMENT FORM

A and B agree to set the number at _____.

A and B agree that, from the award, $ _____ should be paid

from _____ to _____.

Signed _____
                    A

          _____
                    B

EXPERIMENT 17: BEANS AS A MEDIUM OF EXCHANGE

OVERVIEW

The following experiment is designed to simulate an environment where something that is very similar to fiat money will be accepted in market transactions and thus will have a "value."[1] Under a multiproduct trading system, in which students exchange real goods based on their own personal preferences, beans evolve as an efficient medium of exchange.

MATERIALS NEEDED

- A variety of food items
- Transaction record sheets
- A die

ADMINISTERING THE EXPERIMENT

Prior to your classroom lecture on money announce to your students that they are in for a surprise at the next class: you will be serving food instead of the usual lecture.

Divide the class into groups of two to four students and distribute the various food items to each group (see the Appendices at the end of this experiment for a list of food items that might be distributed to a class of twenty-five students). The initial endowments should be distributed so that complementary products will not end up in the hands of the same group of students or the same individual. This guarantees that some exchange will take place before the food is consumed. For example, if one student gets a chef's salad, then another student should get the salad dressing. The total amount of food distributed should be enough to feed the entire class so that nobody goes away unhappy. Furthermore, it is important that beans are in the endowment of some of these groups (for example, groups 3 and 6).

Have your students arrange their chairs so that each group's food endowment is clearly visible to all. Tell your students that they can consume whatever they desire and that there is enough food for everyone in the class. Emphasize that their initial food endowment is such that they will have to trade part of their supply for other items in order to consume it. Explain that they are allowed to make whatever trade they desire and that the exchange rate is negotiable and should be determined by participating groups. Inform the students that they are not allowed to buy or sell on credit. That is, they cannot get a bagel today and tell their classmates that they

---

[1]This is an edited version of an experiment that Harold Fried and Daniel Levy contributed to the Spring, 1992, issue of *Classroom Expernomics*.

will pay for it tomorrow. Also, there is no storage technology, so the students must return any unused items to the instructor.

The transaction period is divided into several subperiods, perhaps five. It is critical that the number of subperiods planned be kept secret from the students. The students are not allowed to eat until after the end of the last subperiod. Each subperiod lasts two to three minutes. At the beginning of the first subperiod announce that at the end of the first subperiod every group will have to pay a certain number of beans as a tax. This makes beans valuable. Inform the groups that you will also collect a tax at the end of every other subperiod, but the amount of the tax will be determined at the end of each subperiod. One way of determining the tax would be to roll a die. Students will need to form expectations about the amount of the tax they will have to pay by estimating the probability of each possible outcome. Students are ejected from the experiment if they do not have enough beans to pay the tax. The experiment ends by closing the market unexpectedly at the end of the fifth subperiod.

Each student or group of students is given a record sheet (found in the Appendices at the end of this experiment) to record their initial endowment of food along with their final endowment, every trade they make, which goods were involved, what the quantities were, and what the exchange rate was. This information is used for the follow-up discussion. The entire simulation, including the dining time, usually takes about forty-five to fifty minutes. If time is a concern, the experiment can be shortened by reducing the number of groups, the number of subperiods, or the number of food items used.

DISCUSSION

Begin your follow-up discussion by soliciting student observations about the experiment. What did they observe or notice that was unique about the trading? Focus the remaining discussion on the functions (medium of exchange, store of value, unit of account), characteristics (homogeneity, divisibility, storability, durability, scarcity), and role of money in an exchange economy.

Since the government (that is, the instructor) accepts tax payments only in the form of beans, beans begin to take on value, and after two or three periods, exchange rates tend to be quoted in terms of beans. Thus, beans start to function as a medium of exchange as well as a unit of account. If the experiment is lengthened to six or seven subperiods, beans may even begin to function as a store of value in the sense that students will start accumulating more beans than they expect they will need to pay taxes. Obviously, if the students know the number of subperiods, they can "rationally" determine the amount of beans they need to accumulate for their future expected taxes. If this happens, beans will have no value beyond the future expected taxes.

A number of variations are possible. Levy and Bergen (1993) describe a setup essentially the same as this one except that they do not provide any beans to the groups. The resulting trades take place under a barter system. The follow-up discussion can then concentrate on the inefficiencies of a barter system and what would be the desirable characteristics of a common medium of exchange.

The present experiment can also be extended to simulate an economy with inflation/deflation by adjusting the quantity of beans accordingly. For example, the instructor can illustrate the impact of an expansionary monetary policy by conducting an open market purchase of tofu using new money (beans). The experiment can also be used to simulate the inflationary effects of a budget deficit by giving every group fifty new beans as a transfer payment.

QUESTIONS

1. What characteristics of beans make them an efficient medium of exchange?

    [Beans are durable, divisible, portable, and scarce.]

2. What impact would an increase in the number of beans have on prices and the number of transactions?

    [The increase in the number of beans is equivalent to an increase in the money supply. According to the quantity theory of money, we would expect that the nominal prices of all items would tend to rise.]

REFERENCES/FURTHER READING

Fried, Harold O., and Daniel Levy. "Beans as a Medium of Exchange." <u>Classroom Expernomics</u> (Spring 1992): 4.

Levy, Daniel, and Mark Bergen. "Simulating A Multiproduct Barter Exchange Economy." <u>Economic Inquiry</u> (April 1993): 314-21.

Radford, R. A. "The Economics of a P.O.W. Camp." <u>Economica</u> (November 1945): 189-201.

APPENDICES TO EXPERIMENT 17

- Menu and initial endowment allocation for a 25-student class
- Transaction record sheet

MENU AND INITIAL ENDOWMENT ALLOCATION FOR A 25-STUDENT CLASS

Group #1
2 tuna salad sandwiches
2 ham sandwiches
3 servings of lasagna
3 plastic spoons

Group #2
Ice cream (one quart)
16 oz. tofu
3 plastic spoons

Group #3
2 chef's salad
3 plastic spoons
100 beans

Group #4
25 plastic plates
25 plastic knives, 3 spoons, 25 forks
Cookies

Group #5
Ice cubes in a plastic bag
Salad dressing (24 servings)
Cream cheese (6 packs, 8 oz each)
3 plastic spoons

Group #6
8 bagels (various flavors)
10 plastic cups
3 plastic spoons
80 beans

Group #7
2 chef's salads
3 two liter Diet Coca-Cola
3 two liter Coca-Cola Classic
3 plastic spoons

Group #8
Napkins (pack of 50)
Pizza (8 slice pie)
4 plastic spoons

Experiment 17

TRANSACTION RECORD SHEET

Name(s) of student(s): _____ _____

_____ _____

Endowment:	Final Consumption:	Leftover:
_____	_____	_____
_____	_____	_____
_____	_____	_____
_____	_____	_____
_____	_____	_____
_____	_____	_____
_____	_____	_____

Initial number of beans _____   No. beans, end of period 1 _____

No. beans, end of period 2 _____   No. beans, end of period 3 _____

No. beans, end of period 4 _____   No. beans, end of period 5 _____

No. Beans, end of period 6 _____   No. beans, end of period 7 _____

Transaction List:

	Type and Quantity of Good Sold	Type and Quantity of Good Bought	Exchange Rate
1.			
2.			
3.			
4.			
5.			
6.			
7.			
8.			

EXPERIMENT 18: A DOUBLE ORAL AUCTION BOND MARKET EXPERIMENT

OVERVIEW

This experiment adapts the double oral auction to a bond market for the purpose of illustrating to students the inverse relationship between bond prices and interest rates.[1] Although students must buy and sell bonds using dollar prices, they are required to convert their reservation and actual buying and selling prices into reservation and actual interest rates.

MATERIALS NEEDED

- Student instructions
- Record sheets
- Cards that inform each student of his or her role as buyer or seller and his or her reservation buying or selling price

ADMINISTERING THE EXPERIMENT

Begin the experiment by distributing the instructions and the record sheets (found in the "Appendices" at the end of this experiment), and cards containing the reservation prices to the students. Read through the instructions, answering any questions that students have about the exercise. You may wish to emphasize that the buyers of the bonds in this market are actually *suppliers* of loanable funds and that the sellers of bonds are actually *demanders* of loanable funds. Buyers and sellers are assigned reservation prices (which can be converted into corresponding reservation interest rates) from Table 1.

This exercise proceeds in the same manner as the standard double oral auction experiment (see Experiment 4). Buyers and sellers orally announce bids and asks (in dollars), and a transaction is made when a buyer or seller accepts an outstanding ask or bid. At the end of each market period, buyers and sellers convert their reservation prices and the dollar prices at which they have bought or sold bonds into reservation and actual interest rates, illustrating the negative relationship between bond prices and interest rates.

---

[1]This is an expanded version of an experiment that David Gillette contributed to the Spring, 1993, issue of *Classroom Expernomics*.

Buyer	Reservation Price	Reservation Interest Rate	Seller	Reservation Price	Reservation Interest Rate
1	$971.25	2.96%	1	$915.00	9.29%
2	$967.50	3.36%	2	$922.00	8.40%
3	$963.75	3.76%	3	$930.00	7.53%
4	$960.00	4.17%	4	$937.50	6.67%
5	$956.25	4.58%	5	$945.00	5.82%
6	$952.50	4.99%	6	$952.50	4.99%
7	$948.75	5.40%	7	$960.00	4.17%
8	$945.00	5.82%	8	$967.50	3.36%
9	$941.25	6.24%	9	$975.00	2.56%
10	$937.50	6.67%	10	$982.50	1.78%
11	$933.75	7.10%	11	$990.00	1.01%
12	$930.00	7.53%	12	$997.00	0.25%
13	$926.25	7.96%	13	$1,005.00	-0.50%
14	$922.50	8.40%	14	$1,012.50	-1.23%
15	$918.75	8.84%	15	$1,020.00	-1.96%
16	$915.00	9.29%	16	$1,027.50	-2.68%
17	$911.25	9.74%	17	$1,035.00	-3.38%
18	$907.50	10.19%	18	$1,042.50	-4.08%

Table 1

DISCUSSION

This simple exercise provides students with a bit of experience in converting dollar bond prices into interest rates, and in so doing illustrates the negative relationship between them. As a slightly more ambitious variation, students could be provided only with their reservation interest rates, but required to tender bids and ask in dollars. This would require that they make the interest rate/price conversion prior to entering the market. If each buyer or seller were to be given the opportunity to buy or sell multiple bonds (each with its own reservation price) in each market period, it would drive home the fact that the lower (higher) a buyer's (seller's) reservation interest rate, the higher (lower) the price at which they would be willing to buy (sell) a bond.

QUESTIONS

1. How did your reservation interest rate vary with your reservation bond price?

    [For buyers, the higher the reservation bond price, the lower the reservation interest rate. For sellers, the lower the reservation bond price, the higher the reservation interest rate.]

REFERENCES/FURTHER READING

Gillette, David. "Bond Markets in Money and Banking." Classroom Expernomics (Spring 1993): 2.

APPENDICES TO EXPERIMENT 18

- Student instructions
- Record sheets

STUDENT INSTRUCTIONS

You are about to participate in an economic experiment concerning the determination of prices and quantities of bonds exchanged in a competitive market structure for corporate bonds. The market structure used in this experiment is known as a "double-oral auction." This means that both bond buyers (i.e., households with money which they want to lend) and bond sellers (i.e., firms with investment projects which they want to finance) orally communicate their desires to the market and this information is known to all market participants. Because the bond market, like every market, has two sides, the class will be divided into two groups, bond buyers (i.e., suppliers of loanable funds) and bond sellers (i.e., demanders of loanable funds). Individual buyers (i.e., households) will attempt to buy bonds from individual sellers (i.e., firms). Everyone in the class will receive a card that is marked "buyer" (supplier or household) or "seller" (demander or firm). The card also contains information about your individual economic limits and desires (constraints). This is your private information; you are not to share it with anyone. You can use this information to make exchanges in the market that will earn profits for you. Your objective as a buyer or seller is to make as much profit as possible. How you can use the information on the card to earn profits is explained below. For simplicity, all bonds will have a face value of $1,000, a maturity of one year, and a coupon payment of zero.

Buyers

Each buyer card contains a number which is your reservation price (i.e., the *maximum* price that you are willing to pay for the bond being issued by the firm with which you are negotiating. This reservation price corresponds to a reservation interest rate and represents your willingness to lend your money to any firm in the market. Enter this value in the appropriate column of your record sheet. As a buyer (household) you will be making bids to buy bonds (lend money) in the bond market. You can make a bid to lend money for any price you wish as long as it is less than the price listed on your card. (For example, if your card says $950.00 your could buy a bond for $925.00 but not for $960.00. Note that these numbers are only used as an example; check your own card for your personal limit.) An officer of the SEC will be checking to insure that you do not make an illegal transaction. Buyer profit will be determined by the highest average interest earnings. Thus to make the most profit, you need to lend money for the highest interest rate possible.

Sellers

Each seller card contains a number which is your reservation price (i.e., the *minimum* price for which you are willing to sell the bond being purchased by the household with which you are negotiating). This reservation price corresponds to your reservation interest rate and represents your willingness to borrow money from any household in the market and is determined by the investment demand schedule which you face as a firm. Enter this price in the appropriate column of your record sheet. As a seller (firm) you will be making bids to sell bonds (borrow money) in the bond market. You can make a bid to sell bonds at any price you wish as long as it is greater than the price listed on your card. (For example, if your card says $950.00 you could borrow money at $960.00 but not at $925.00. Note that these numbers are only used as an example; check your own card for your own personal limit.) An officer of the SEC will be checking to insure that you do not make an illegal transaction. Seller profit will be determined by the lowest average interest expenses. Thus to make the most profit, you need to borrow money at the lowest interest rate possible.

Making Transactions

Since all trades will be negotiated in dollar prices and not interest rates, it will be necessary for you to calculate your reservation interest rate and your interest earnings. Recall that you can do this by using the following formula:

$$PV = FV/(1+i)$$

where *PV*, the present value, is the price of the bond and *FV*, the future value, is the face value of the bond, in this case $1,000.

In a double-oral auction, buyers and sellers simultaneously make their wishes known to the other market participants. Buyers will shout out their bids to buy and sellers will shout out their offers to sell. In this bond market experiment, that means buyers shout out the prices they are willing to pay for a bond (the lower the better) and sellers shout out the prices for which they are willing to sell their bonds (the higher the better). Each buyer and seller can make only one transaction in each trading period. When an acceptance is made on your bid or offer, the pit boss (that is, your instructor) will record the transaction and you drop out of the market until the next trading period. The length of the trading period is determined by the pit boss. The pit boss may stop the trading at the end of each period with a "soft close" which means that buyers will be asked if they will accept the last offer and sellers will be asked if they will accept the last bid. When no acceptances are forthcoming, the period will end. The number of trading periods in this experiment will be determined by the pit boss.

Remember, as an individual market participant, you are interested in maximizing your own economic position. This means making the most profit that you can on each transaction. It is always better to make a transaction than not to make a transaction (a little profit is better than no profit!). The buyer and seller that performs the best throughout the experiment will be rewarded in an economic fashion!

Good luck !

RECORD SHEETS

Buyer	Round 1	Round 2	Round 3	Round 4	Round 5
Reservation Price					
Purchase Price					
Buyer's Profit					

Seller	Round 1	Round 2	Round 3	Round 4	Round 5
Sale Price					
Reservation Price					
Seller's Profit					

Buyer	Round 1	Round 2	Round 3	Round 4	Round 5
Reservation Interest Rate					
Negotiated Interest Rate					
Buyer's Int. Earnings					

Seller	Round 1	Round 2	Round 3	Round 4	Round 5
Negotiated Interest Rate					
Reservation Interest Rate					
Seller's Int. Payment					

BIBLIOGRAPHY

Beck, John H. "An Experimental Test of Preferences for the Distribution of Income." Classroom Expernomics (Spring 1992): 2-3.

Bishop, Jerry E. "All for One...One for All? Don't Bet on It." Wall Street Journal (December 4, 1986): 37.

Brock, John R. "A Public Goods Experiment For The Classroom." Economic Inquiry (April 1991): 395-401.

_____. "Experimental Derivation of a Demand Curve." Classroom Expernomics (Fall 1992): 3-4.

Davis, Douglas D., and Charles Holt. Experimental Economics. Princeton University Press, 1993.

Field, Barry C. Environmental Economics. McGraw-Hill, 1994.

Fried, Harold O., and Daniel Levy. "Beans as a Medium of Exchange." Classroom Expernomics (Spring 1992): 4.

Friedman, Daniel, and Shyam Sunder. Experimental Methods: A Primer for Economists. Cambridge University Press, 1994.

Gardner, Roy. Games For Business And Economics. John Wiley & Sons, Inc., 1995.

Gillette, David. "Bond Markets in Money and Banking." Classroom Expernomics (Spring 1993): 2.

Haupert, Michael J. "Sunk Cost and Marginal Cost." Classroom Expernomics (Spring 1994): 6-7.

Hemenway, David, Robert Moore, and James Whitney. "The Oligopoly Game." Economic Inquiry (October 1987): 727-730.

Hoffman, Elizabeth, and Matthew Spitzer. "The Coase Theorem: Some Experimental Tests." Journal of Law and Economics (1982), 73-98.

Leuthold, Jane H. "A Free-Rider Experiment for the Large Class." Journal of Economic Education (Fall 1993): 353-63.

Levy, Daniel, and Mark Bergen. "Simulating A Multiproduct Barter Exchange Economy." Economic Inquiry (April 1993): 314-21.

Neral, John, and Margaret Ray. "Experiential Learning in the Undergraduate Classroom: Two Exercises." Economic Inquiry (January 1995): 170-174.

Passell, Peter. "Cheapest Protection of Nature May Lie in Taxes, Not Laws." New York Times (November 24, 1994): B5.

Radford, R. A. "The Economics of a P.O.W. Camp." Economica (November 1945): 189-201.

Roberts, Russell D. The Choice: A Fable of Free Trade and Protectionism. Prentice Hall, 1994.

Smith, Vernon L. "An Experimental Study of Competitive Market Behavior." Journal of Political Economy (April 1962): 111-137.

_____. "Markets as Economizers of Information: Experimental Examination of the 'Hayek Hypothesis'." Economic Inquiry (1982): 165-179.

_____. "Microeconomic Systems as an Experimental Science." American Economic Review (December 1982): 923-955.

Stodder, Jim. "A Simple Experiment of Comparative Advantage." Classroom Expernomics (Spring 1994): 8-10.

Taylor, Jeffrey. "New Rules Harness Power of Free Markets to Curb Air Pollution." Wall Street Journal (April 14, 1992): A1.

Tietenberg, Tom. Emissions Trading. Johns Hopkins University Press for Resources for the Future, 1985.

Weidenaar, Dennis. "A Classroom Experiment Demonstrating the Generation of a Market Demand Function and the Determination of Equilibrium Price." Journal of Economic Education (Spring 1972): 94-100.

Wells, Donald A. "Laboratory Experiments for Undergraduate Instruction in Economics." Journal of Economic Education (Summer 1991): 293-300.

Williams, Arlington W., and James M. Walker. "Computerized Laboratory Exercises for Microeconomics Education: Three Applications Motivated by Experimental Economics." Journal of Economic Education (Fall 1993): 291-315.